TWILIGHT PRISONERS

TWILIGHT PRISONERS

THE RISE OF THE HINDU RIGHT AND THE FALL OF INDIA

SIDDHARTHA DEB

Haymarket Books
Chicago, IL

© 2024 Siddhartha Deb
Published in 2024 by
Haymarket Books
P.O. Box 180165
Chicago, IL 60618
www.haymarketbooks.org

ISBN: 979-8-88890-126-7

Distributed to the trade in the US through Consortium Book Sales and Distribution (www.cbsd.com) and internationally through Ingram Publisher Services International (www.ingramcontent.com).

This book was published with the generous support of Lannan Foundation, Wallace Action Fund, and Marguerite Casey Foundation.

Special discounts are available for bulk purchases by organizations and institutions. Please email info@haymarketbooks.org for more information.

Cover artwork by Raghu Rai / Magnum Photos.
Cover design by David Gee.

Library of Congress Cataloging-in-Publication data is available.

Entered into digital printing in February 2024.

Contents

Introduction — 1

Part I
1. Nowhere Man: The Violence, Rage, and Insecurity of Narendra Modi — 13
2. An Alien Visitation: The Worst Industrial Disaster in the History of the World — 45
3. Nowhere Land: The Lost Dissidents of Manipur — 61

Part II
4. Manufacturing Foreigners: India's War of Disenfranchisement against Muslims — 87
5. Ram's Kingdom: The Ayodhya Temple and the Ruins of History — 107
6. Impossible Machines: Vimanas and Hindu-Right Fantasies of Ancient Technology — 139

Part III
7. Killing Gauri Lankesh: Political Assassinations and the Silencing of Dissident Voices — 157
8. Manufacturing Evidence: The Bhima Koregaon Conspiracy and the Plot to Imprison India's Activists — 175
9. The Renegade at the Nation's Gates: Arundhati Roy and the Politics of Prose — 19

Acknowledgments — 207
Previously Published — 209
Index — 211

*For those who listen to their hearts and who act
on the belief that better worlds are possible.*

Introduction

One recent summer morning, I found myself looking for an Indian city that appeared to have vanished. I was in Delhi, arriving there not long after a brutal wave of the pandemic had sent even well-to-do Indians scrambling for oxygen cylinders and hospital beds. Now, as the public health crisis seemed all but forgotten, I made plans to travel to the North Indian state of Uttar Pradesh, epicenter of the pandemic and heartland of Hindu nationalism. In order to orient myself as I worked out a tentative route from Delhi on Google Maps, I looked for the city of Allahabad, one of the oldest and most significant cities in Uttar Pradesh, sited on the banks of the notionally sacred, and utterly polluted, Ganges River. It wasn't there.

Once an important locus of India's anti-colonial struggle, home to the Nehru family that produced three prime ministers in postcolonial India, Allahabad had entered a period of decline decades ago. But decline is one thing, disappearance another. How was it possible that a city of 1.8 million people could have ceased to exist without my hearing a word about it? But there was no Allahabad on Google Maps, no matter what I tried. Instead, occupying what looked suspiciously like the same pixelated spot on the screen, was "Prayagraj," an entity I'd never heard of before.

Clarity came, eventually, accompanied by a sinking feeling. Allahabad, founded by the sixteenth-century Mughal emperor Akbar, had been renamed for its notionally Islamic associations, and in a perfect convergence between Hindu nationalism and global capitalism, the new Hindu nomenclature had been made official by Google. History had been rewritten, and barely anyone had noticed.

The erasure of the past and the rewriting of the present is a feature everywhere in our embattled times. But its most powerful, and its most successful iteration is in India under the Hindu-right government led by Narendra Modi. Unnoticed by the West because of its hubris as epicenter, whether of history or of the end of history, the mythmaking unleashed by Hindu nationalism in India has achieved almost total success, transforming material as well as virtual reality. Dominating the physical landscape while also taking possession of the hearts and minds of a significant section of its population, it is the most successful right-wing phenomenon of our times, bridging Western fascism from the early twentieth century with the multiple, overlapping, digitally inflected authoritarianisms of our era.

This should not be surprising. Hindu nationalism is unrivaled in its capacity to bide its time; it outlasted the colonialism with which it collaborated during British rule; it outlasted, too, the Nehruvian decades of decolonization during which it lurked in the slimy undercurrents of political life. It emerged into the open only when the moment was right, at the turn of the twenty-first century, when the left had been defeated globally and the market ruled over all. During that dawn of the new millennium—a new millennium that now, just at the beginning of its third decade, already feels tired, old, and disorienting—Hindu nationalism came into its own. As the country was eviscerated by capital both Western and domestic, erasing all memory of left, anti-colonial, and Third World ideals, stamping out any sense of alternatives to a homogeneous, soulless globalization, Hindu nationalism inserted a mythical past that would offer a sense of belonging even as the plunder went on. The high-rises and the highways, the rich in their towers and the poor dispersed everywhere were, it insisted, not just weak simulacra of the monochromatic world being ushered in globally, but the trace of something unique, a Hindu utopia stirring into life after millennia of oppression.

This was the promise embodied by Modi as the most eloquent representation of Hindu nationalism when he became prime minister in 2014. Handed an even more resounding electoral victory five years later, in 2019, he moved swiftly to further this Hindu utopia by changing the constitutional status of Muslim-majority Kashmir, by revising India's citizenship law in such a way that only Muslims were affected, and by rushing to complete the construction of a massive temple to the Hindu god Ram in Ayodhya, a small pilgrimage town in Uttar Pradesh. At the height of the pandemic—to which his government had responded primarily with a lockdown that sent millions of low-wage workers back to their villages on foot as they attempted to outwalk starvation—he appeared in Ayodhya to lay the foundation stone of the temple, the event broadcast live onto a billboard in New York's Times Square.

In spite of a stuttering economy and the precariousness that had been starkly made visible by the pandemic, Hindu nationalism retained the sense that its time is now. It was in order to understand that triumphal sense of a toxic nationalism arriving at its moment, to investigate its claims that the outline of a Hindu utopia was being put in place, that I traveled to Ayodhya that summer, an account of which appears in this book.

§

I have been writing about Hindu nationalism and India for a very long time. My first freelance piece for a Western publication—"Banned in Benares" for the now defunct *Lingua Franca*—covered the Hindu right's attack on the historian D. N. Jha for his meticulously researched monograph *Holy Cow: Beef in Indian Dietary Traditions*. That piece, however, appeared in November 2001, shortly after the terror attacks of 9/11. In the coming months and years, the eye of Western media would focus not on Hindu fundamentalism but on Islamic fundamentalism. This was the great enemy that had emerged from the thawing that followed the Cold War, the new scourge of democracy and of markets. Hindu fundamentalism was a sideshow in this Manichean conflict, a minor feature in a nation turning out to be a useful ally in the new global war on terror. I saw this in the reactions of some of the white editors who took me out to lunch —vaguely well-meaning, puzzled by my denunciations of the market, India, and Hindu nationalism, their fleeting anxieties about the Hindu right's links with European fascism and the Nazis papered over by its solidly anti-Communist, market-friendly, and yogic credentials.

It wasn't just the Western media. The Indian elite—mostly upper-caste, upper-class, Hindu—in positions of power in technology, finance, media, and publishing stayed quiet through those decades. With the notable exception of Arundhati Roy and Pankaj Mishra, no major Indian writer with access to Western platforms thought it worthwhile to critique either Hindu nationalism or the market forces that together were beginning to transform India into a dystopia. A genocidal massacre of Muslims in Gujarat in 2002, where Modi had just become the chief minister, was more or less allowed to vanish from memory as India became the ideal non-Western nation, an entire nation playing the role of a model minority. As a fierce scourge of Islamic fundamentalism and rival to China and Pakistan, and as a wildly enthusiastic convert to capitalism, India was the right kind of rising power.

My last nonfiction book, *The Beautiful and the Damned* (2011), was a counter-narrative to this account and an exploration of the nexus between Hindu nationalism and neoliberalism, and of the violence lurking underneath the techno-shine of consumerist Delhi and Bangalore. It was an outlier. A glut of India books, articles, and talks, whether by Indians, diaspora Indians from the UK and the US, or white, Western experts jetting in and out of the new airports, offered wildly enthusiastic, improbable accounts of a new India that had finally awakened from decades of postcolonial sloth. "The East is a career," the nineteenth-century British leader Benjamin Disraeli had said (it serves as an epigraph in Edward Said's *Orientalism*); in the glow of the new millennium, lit up by cluster bombs coming down on Afghanistan and Iraq, India was a racket, thriving at literary festivals and leadership summits, at business conferences and university panels.

The national election in 2014 that made Modi prime minister did not change the thriving careers of those working in the India industry. He was enthusiastically welcomed on the national and world stage, including by liberals who relentlessly attacked Roy and Mishra—and me as well—for their naivete and disconnect from India's arrival into glory. It was only after Modi's second electoral victory in 2019, when the war against Islamic fundamentalism had begun to fade from the public discourse, when globalization lay in tatters under Trump and Brexit, and when India's mask of promise had slipped off completely to reveal billionaire oligarchs, Hindu nationalist thugs, and a dysfunctional economy, that a few India and Modi boosters began to reinvent themselves as longtime critics of Modi.

The Western powers nevertheless remained steadfast in their admiration for Modi and his political party. In the summer of 2023, as the air quality in New York briefly resembled that in New Delhi, Modi appeared on a state visit in Washington. The welcome from Joseph Biden was consistent with previous overtures from Barack Obama in 2016 and by Donald Trump in 2019. Addressing a joint session of Congress after being serenaded at the White House with an a capella rendition of a Bollywood number, Modi went home satisfied, freshly recertified as a democratic leader by the US and with a defense deal for thirty-one Predator "hunter-killer" drones in his pocket.

§

This book is an account of this past decade and a half and the pivot from seeming promise to undeniable disaster. A collection of essays and reported pieces, it is a narrative of how a nation and a culture widely celebrated as a success story at the turn of the century suddenly revealed itself to be an authoritarian dystopia, how what was called India Shining in the new millennium became a perpetual, pollution-laced twilight. But while this book is about India, it is also about much more. It shows that India should be understood neither as part of the rising industrial-capitalist complex of Brazil Russia India China (BRIC) nor as a late but diligent newcomer to the Anglo-American capitalist democratic system that is the seeming endpoint of history. It instead reveals how India is connected to Russia and to the United States, to Brazil and to Britain—not in terms of trickle-down prosperity, but in how they all mirror, with variations, toxic nationalism, environmental disaster, precarity ranging from the middle classes down to destitution for those at the very bottom of the social ladder, and a degraded media-arts-entertainment-education apparatus whose loud, constant outpour conceals its utter lack of original thought and empathy.

We start with Narendra Modi and his rise from obscurity as a Hindu-right paramilitary member to world leader. This is followed by two pieces about the convenient negation of memory that formed a prehistory to the project of complete erasure being carried out by the Hindu right today; the first is about Bhopal, site of the 1984 industrial disaster that stands as the worst such incident in world history, conveniently forgotten by Union Carbide, Dow Chemical, and elites in India and the United States (there will never be an HBO show called *Bhopal*); the second is about a hidden camp of Burmese dissidents in Manipur in northeast India, people who were invited across the border by the Indian government in an initial show of democratic solidarity and who were then vilified and abandoned when they became an inconvenience to the geopolitical ambitions of rising India.

The second section is about the mythologies constructed by the Hindu right as it deftly exploited modern technologies, media, market forces, and violence both state-sanctioned and freelance. This begins with a piece on the detention centers in the state of Assam, where the Hindu right channeled local grievances about a porous border into the myth that millions of foreigners were taking over the region, producing a terrifying, carceral regime that stripped a million Bengali-speaking Muslims of their Indian citizenship while imprisoning countless others. It is followed by an account of my journey to Ayodhya in the summer of 2021 to visit the Ram temple being constructed as the centerpiece of a future Hindu utopia—Ramrajya, or "Ram's Kingdom"—that will mirror a fantastic past that never existed. The last piece in this section is an essay on the fantasies of ancient Vedic aircraft and how its modern origins are concurrent with colonialism and the beginning of Hindu nationalism.

The final section is about the resistance to Hindu nationalism. This includes figures such as the journalist Gauri Lankesh, assassinated by a foot soldier of the Hindu right in 2017; the BK16, a group of activists, thinkers, and writers incarcerated under concocted anti-terror charges since 2018; and Arundhati Roy, whose distinctive trajectory as a writer has involved engaging with politics as well as aesthetics, with writing nonfiction as well as fiction while resisting both Hindu nationalism and global capitalism.

The pieces presented in this collection—some are essays and some are reported pieces—also attempt that intersection of politics and aesthetics, just as they try to show that Hindu nationalism and global capitalism reinforce and feed off each other. Narrative quests, as much as they are political and investigative queries, are meant for the engaged general reader, with those interested in imaginative possibilities as well as in stark material realities. The pieces here are also in conversation with my fiction, particularly my novel, *The Light at the End of the World*, an echoing and mirroring that sometimes takes on haunting overtones, as in my visit to a detention center in Assam in 2021—years after Bibi, the protagonist of my novel, had undertaken a similar journey of her own.

§

What this book offers, then, is an account of this darkest of turns in India's history. Because everything happens so fast—"one single catastrophe piling wreckage upon wreckage," as Walter Benjamin wrote—this book is an attempt to slow things down, to put things on the record, to show that Modi was every bit as reprehensible in 2002 as he eventually turned out to be for some of his liberal admirers in 2019, that the market was not a gateway to greater equality and democracy in India but a hall of mirrors distracting us from cruelties new and old pulsating through the land. It is a report from the frontiers of the unraveling of India's flawed national project, an account of the multitudes who are prisoners as its midnight promise of decolonization and Third World liberation (what Nehru extolled as "Freedom at Midnight" as India became a nation on the midnight of August 15, 1947) transforms into the bitter twilight of oligarchy, authoritarianism, and climate collapse. Most of all, it is meant to show that those multitudes—those who suffered and are suffering, those who resisted and are resisting—are not forgotten. As long as there is resistance and remembrance, there is still hope.

PART I

Chapter 1
Nowhere Man

The Violence, Rage, and Insecurity of Narendra Modi

In September 2014, at Madison Square Garden in New York, India's prime minister, Narendra Modi, addressed a crowd of nearly 20,000 people.* It was a sold-out spectacle worthy of a lush Bollywood production, with dancers warming up the audience and giant screens flashing portraits of Modi in the style of Shepard Fairey's 2008 Barack Obama "Hope" poster. There was a revolving stage, a speed portrait painter, and a bipartisan coterie of American politicians, including senators Chuck Schumer and

---

* First published in the *New Republic*, June 2016. On June 8, 2016, Modi addressed a joint session of the Congress. In a discussion on NPR, Alyssa Ayres, former Obama official and a fellow at the Council of Foreign Relations, defended Modi and India, describing my critique as unfair to a "fledgling" democracy. In September 2019, Modi appeared at the NRG stadium in Texas with Trump for a "Howdy Modi" rally. In July 2023, Modi was invited by Biden on a state visit to Washington. Shortly after, on July 14, he appeared in Paris as a guest of honor at the Bastille Day parade. A photo session with Emmanuel Macron in front of the Mona Lisa was apparently on the schedule, as well as finalizing a deal for the sale of 26 Rafale fighter aircraft and three Scorpene submarines to India, by now the largest arms importer in the world.

Robert Menendez, and South Carolina governor Nikki Haley who is of Indian descent.

When Modi appeared, dressed in saffron, a color associated with the ascetic, martial traditions of Hinduism, his first words were "*Bharat Mata Ki,*" an invocation of India as a Hindu goddess that translates as "For Mother India." The crowd, almost entirely Indian American, some with Hindu *tikas* dotting their foreheads, finished the line for him. "*Jai!*" (Victory!) they shouted. "*Bharat Mata Ki Jai!*" Then they broke out into the chant, "Modi, Modi, Modi!"

Modi's hourlong speech touched on every element of the received wisdom about India as a vibrant democracy and rising economic power. He spoke of its special prowess in information technology and the particular role played by Indian Americans in this. He spoke of India's youthful population, with 65 percent of its billion-plus people under thirty-five; of Make in India, a program that encapsulated his plans to transform the country into a manufacturing powerhouse along the lines of China; and the ways in which his humble origins and meteoric political ascent served as an example of what might be possible in India today.

This address was followed by many similar ones around the world, but it was the first to establish on a global stage an idea that had been doing the rounds, in India, in the Indian diaspora, and among Western nations keen to carry out business in India: Modi and India were versions of each other, doppelgängers marching through the world and conveying a new era. Even Barack Obama made the comparison, writing in *Time*'s annual list of the hundred most influential people in the world: "As a boy, Narendra Modi helped his father sell tea to support their family. Today, he's the leader of the world's largest democracy, and his life story—from poverty to prime minister—reflects the dynamism and potential of India's rise."

Dynamism, potential, rise: these are the states of being captured by the entwinement of India and Modi. In the minds of India's elite, and in that of an admiring, supportive West, India has been rising for a while, ever since it fully embraced Western capitalism in the early 1990s. Modi's Madison Square Garden appearance was but an expression of that ascendance, from slumdogs into millionaires. But Modi was also in New York because of something that accompanies the rising India narrative: the perplexing reality that, having been rising for so long, India is still not risen.

In the past fifteen years, the top 1 percent of earners in India have increased their share of the country's wealth from 36.8 percent to 53 percent, with the top 10 percent owning 76.3 percent, and yet India remains a stunningly poor country, riven with violence and brutal hierarchies, held together with shoddy infrastructure, and marked by the ravages of lopsided growth, pollution, and climate change. Modi at Madison Square Garden, then, stood for the promise that India's rise would finally be completed, the summit reached. It had not yet been achieved, but he would change that. He would change it because he was an outsider, a man of humble origins, leading a political party—the Hindu-right Bharatiya Janata Party (BJP)—that had a few months earlier been given a clear electoral majority, the first time for any Indian party in thirty years. He was at Madison Square Garden to mark this triumph, and to declare himself the new Indian icon for a new Indian century.

Modi referred, naturally, to the icon he had supplanted, the one from a previous century. Stumbling over Gandhi's first name, calling him "Mohanlal" instead of "Mohandas," Modi compared Gandhi to the members of his audience, as a person who had lived abroad as a diaspora Indian before returning to India. Modi's Gandhi, however, had nothing to do with anti-colonial politics, mysticism, or nonviolence. Those had been left behind with the old India, as demonstrated by some of Modi's supporters outside the venue. Gathered in large numbers, they heckled and jeered at the Indian television anchor Rajdeep Sardesai for being part of what they saw as the liberal wing of the Indian media, which is ill disposed toward Modi. To Sardesai's attempts to ask them questions, they responded with shouts of "Modi, Modi, Modi." When he retorted, "Did Mr. Modi tell you to behave badly? Did America tell you to behave badly?" a brawl ensued, some of the men chanting, "*Vande Mataram!*" or "Praise Mother India!" while others shouted, "Motherfucker!"

This episode could be seen as an aberration, but the combination of adulation and violence, sanctimoniousness and abuse, is never far from Modi and those who support him. It is, in fact, the essence of his appeal. He is a representative Indian not merely because he signifies potential, outsider status, an Indian form of DIY upward mobility, but also because he embodies violent sectarian and authoritarian tendencies: so much a modern man belonging to the new century that he has dispensed with the pacifism associated with Gandhi.

One could see that in the jostling bodies and shouting faces gathered around the Indian television anchor. At work, these clean-cut, middle-class Indian men in their saffron t-shirts displaying Modi's face probably exuded deference and respectability, at least toward those they associated with power and wealth. But gathered in numbers, with their puffed-up chests and clenched fists, they replicated what they admired most about Modi—a kind of unmoored nihilism that dresses itself in religious colors and acts through violence, that is ruthlessly authoritarian in the face of diversity and dissent, and that imprints the brute force of its majoritarianism wherever it is in power.

During his speech, Modi told the crowd the story of an interpreter in Taiwan who had asked him if India was a land of black magic, with snakes and snake charmers. This drew nervous laughter from the men and women in their professional clothes. The story was in a familiar genre, that of the Indian humiliated abroad, and can be found even in Gandhi's accounts of colonialism and racism when traveling to the West. For Gandhi and his contemporaries (and in fact for all colonized, marginalized cultures), that experience of humiliation had led sometimes to a kind of nativism—a reaffirmation of the superior values of one's humiliated society—but it had also provoked an anti-colonialism that was internationalist in spirit, identifying with other marginalized groups.

But Modi was speaking for a new India and to a new India, one obsessed with completing its rise as an economic power. Neither the speaker nor the crowd acknowledged that snake charming in India is an occupation based on caste, and that they were far removed from such livelihoods. They were simply angry and afraid, humiliated that their Indianness could be tainted by such associations, and it is not hard to empathize with that sense of being patronized. But where the anti-colonial, Gandhi-inspired Indian might have worn the snake-charmer tag as a badge of pride, the new, Modi Indian merely wanted it destroyed. The new Indian instinctively understood the point of Modi's anecdote, which was that it was set in Taiwan—not a Western country, but still ahead of India in terms of modernity.

"Our country has become very devalued," Modi said. Cheers resounded through the stadium, the well-dressed professionals at Madison Square Garden united in their common sense of humiliation. Modi waited for the cheers to die down. Then he said, "Our ancestors used to play with snakes. We play with the *mouse*." The applause this time was deafening. In the twist of a metaphor, Modi had restored the honor of the nation and of all those present. India was not a nation of snake charmers but of high-tech mouse managers. And Modi understood this, because he too was an Indian driven by rage and humiliation, a newcomer to the system and a latecomer to modernity, a leader who would transform India into a land of Silicon Valley white magic, but who would retain its authentic Hindu core.

Listening to the crowd finishing off his call-and-response of "*Bharat Mata Ki* … ," he said, "Close both your fists and say it with full strength." The crowd rose, fists clenched, shouting out the promise of triumph, of victory: "*Bharat Mata Ki Jai!*"

§

In 1893, more than a century before Modi appeared at Madison Square Garden, a Hindu preacher called Vivekananda arrived in Chicago. The popular version of the story, as told in India, describes him as a solitary, charismatic figure dressed in saffron robes and turban as he faced the harsh cold and desiccated materialism of the West. The more prosaic, if still dramatic, truth is that Vivekananda had come to attend the World's Parliament of Religions, a sideshow to that year's World's Fair. There were representatives from many religions at the parliament, hoping to speak to a West relentless in the assertion of its double-barreled superiority, as embodied by Western Christianity and the Enlightenment. Soyen Shaku, one of whose students, D. T. Suzuki, became the most famous Zen teacher in the United States, came as part of a Japanese delegation. The Sinhalese preacher Anagarika Dharmapala was to represent Theravada Buddhism. Mohammed Alexander Russell Webb, a former American consul to the Philippines who had converted to Islam, spoke on the faith he had embraced.

Vivekananda was a remarkable, complex figure, introducing a distinct, modernized version of yoga and neo-Hinduism to the

United States. But if his legacy in the West was to be yoga, in India it would morph—helped, no doubt, by his early death at thirty-nine—into a muscular Hindu nationalism centered on the idea that Hindus needed to become more aggressive in challenging both Islam and the West. He became a symbol of the Hindu warrior monk who had gone into the West to conquer it for Hinduism, an idea embodied loudly by Modi in his own self-presentation, especially in the cross-armed pose and saffron turban he affected. And just as Vivekananda, in this populist version, took the battle to the West, so did Modi when he arrived at Madison Square Garden.

In India, it took an organization and the onset of race-based nationalism in the early twentieth century to give Vivekananda's vision a more sinister touch and ultimately connect it to Modi. Founded in 1925 in the central Indian city of Nagpur, the Rashtriya Swayamsevak Sangh (RSS), the National Volunteer Organization, took Vivekananda's ideas of Hindu revival a step further, combining them with racial theories popular in the West and drawing inspiration from the Italian Fascists and the Nazis. M. S. Golwalkar, who became the chief of the RSS in 1940, wrote approvingly of Germany's "purging the country of the Semitic Races—the Jews," and urged Hindus to manifest a similar "Race Spirit" with Muslims. After India became independent in 1947, Nathuram Godse, a former member of the RSS, assassinated Gandhi for being too conciliatory toward Muslims and Pakistan. The RSS was banned briefly, but this was a blip in its steady expansion from its base in the western state of Maharashtra into neighboring Gujarat, Modi's home state, and beyond.

The RSS was known for its secretive, cultlike tendencies; it kept no written fundraising records, and it produced a constitution only in 1949 as a condition for the lifting of its ban. It had stayed away from anti-colonial politics under the British and maintained a distance from electoral politics in the decades following independence. It focused, instead, on the ideal of an upper-caste Hindu society within an unabashedly upper-caste, patriarchal Hindu nation. It recruited boys between the ages of six and eighteen, using doctrinaire lectures and a routine of paramilitary drills to mold their Hindu "Race Spirit," while its adult members were unleashed as shock troops in riots against Muslims. It maintained links with Hindu-right political parties and with those leaders from the ruling Indian National Congress who were favorably inclined to its sectarian idea of India, but it avoided direct involvement in parliamentary politics, calling itself a social organization rather than a political one.

This was the organization—disciplined, secretive, tainted by its association with Gandhi's assassination and its role in sectarian riots—that Modi joined in 1958 as an eight-year-old in the provincial Gujarati town of Vadnagar. He was the third of six children, from a family that ran a tea shop at the railway station to supplement its income from pressing and selling cooking oil. Leaving home as a teenager, Modi wandered the country, possibly to escape living with the wife who had been chosen for him in an arranged marriage at an early age—ironically, just the sort of social practice defended by the Hindu right, despite legislative attempts to make marriage and divorce more equitable, especially for Hindu women—and from whom he remains estranged. He returned after a couple of years to the Gujarati city of Ahmedabad, where he briefly ran a tea stall before joining the RSS full-time. Modi soon completed the RSS's one-month officer-training program and became a *pracharak*, or organizer.

One can see the attractions of the RSS for a young man like Modi, filled with ambition and intelligence but without much education or opportunity. Its warrior-monk structure would offer upward mobility and power even as its cultish ideology stoked a sense of humiliation about the place of India in the world, and of Hindus within India. Decades later, when Modi wrote a book entitled *Jyotipunj* (Beams of light) about the people he admired most, his list would consist exclusively of RSS members, foremost among them the Hitler-loving Golwalkar. Modi rose rapidly through the ranks of this organization, one not dissimilar—in its paranoia, violence, and sense of victimization—to the Ku Klux Klan. There were always questions about his egocentrism, such as his tendency to wear a beard rather than the look encouraged by the RSS—military mustache or clean-shaven—and his tendency to upstage his rivals, but he was an efficient organizer in an outfit that needed these skills as it became more directly involved in influencing electoral politics.

The RSS had always maintained a loose affiliation with Hindu political parties. As the BJP emerged in the 1980s as the primary political party of the Hindu right, led by men who were also members of the RSS, that relationship grew stronger, until the BJP, the RSS, and a range of other Hindu-right organizations formed what in India is called the Sangh Parivar, or "Sangh Family." The BJP's task has been to provide the political face of the Sangh Parivar, while the RSS remains its shadowy soul.

The Hindu right, especially the BJP, grew in influence as the Congress, India's main political party, weakened. By the 1980s, the Congress, dominated by the Nehru-Gandhi family, had begun to dabble in sectarian politics and Hindu nationalism. When Indira Gandhi was assassinated by Sikh separatists in 1984, senior Congress leaders, joined by RSS members, directed a pogrom against the Sikh minority that resulted in the death of 2,700 people, according to official estimates. Rajiv Gandhi, the next prime minister, took his mother's sectarian politics further while also beginning India's tilt toward the United States and toward information technology and a market-driven economy. This process would create a new Indian elite that was both aggressive and insecure about its place in the market economy, something it compensated for by reconfiguring itself as narrowly Hindu.

The BJP profited from these trends, using the RSS philosophy of Hindutva (Hindu-ness) plus the slogan, "Say with pride that we're Hindus," to go from 2 seats in the national parliament in 1984 to 85 in 1989, beginning a steady rise that, after a brief dip in 2004 and 2009, culminated in 282 seats, or 51.9 percent of the total, in the 2014 elections that made Modi prime minister.

There were significant opportunities for Modi as the Hindu right expanded its sectarian politics. The first, and most pivotal, campaign of the Hindu right involved a movement in 1990 to rebuild a temple to Ram, the mythological hero of the *Ramayana*, on the disputed site of the Babri Masjid, a sixteenth-century mosque in Ayodhya, in northern India. The BJP leader at the time, L. K. Advani, rode a Toyota truck modified into a "chariot" around the country to rally Hindus to the cause, starting his journey at Somnath in Gujarat, where a temple had been destroyed in the eleventh century by a Central Asian Muslim invader, and traveling toward Babri Masjid.

Modi was RSS general secretary at the time, a position that entailed directing the BJP from behind the scenes, making sure that it was following the RSS's agenda. He organized the opening segment of the tour, and old photographs show him standing next to Advani on the chariot. In a sign of things to come, the temple campaign went global, shored up by other members of the Sangh Family, including the Vishwa Hindu Parishad, or World Hindu Council, which focuses much of its energies on the Indian diaspora in the West. Hindus around the world were asked to donate bricks to build the temple to Ram. Bricks, some made of gold, arrived from abroad as well as from hundreds of villages and towns in India, and although Advani's tour ended when he was arrested for inciting violence, the mobilization continued. On December 6, 1992, Babri Masjid was leveled by a Hindu-right mob, setting off a spiral of violence that resulted in the death of around 2,000 people.

The violence of the Ayodhya campaign, the crude depictions of Muslims as brutal invaders, the deft use of political spectacle, and the targeting of all this toward a new Indian elite both ambitious and insecure were trends that Modi would embrace and develop. In 1995, he became BJP national secretary and moved to Delhi, just as India began its conversion to a full-fledged market economy and embarked on a period of economic growth that would benefit the urban elites enormously. The market, the nation, and Hindutva converged as the BJP won the elections in 1998, the new government carrying out a series of nuclear tests to celebrate the victory. A year later, it fought a brief war with Pakistan. The nuclear tests and the war were promoted hysterically by media outlets that were consumed eagerly by a growing urban elite, drawing in even liberal Indians who might have been uneasy about the Ayodhya campaign but who liked the way this new India asserted itself on the global stage.

§

In October 2001, Modi was appointed chief minister of Gujarat by the BJP leadership in Delhi. It was the first time an RSS *pracharak* had become chief executive of an Indian state. The impact was apparent soon afterward. In February 2002, fifty-nine Hindus returning from the tenth-anniversary celebration of the destruction of the Babri Masjid died in a fire that broke out in a train compartment. Investigations would later point to the fire originating inside the carriage, perhaps from a malfunctioning cooking-gas cylinder, but the Hindu right accused Muslims of storming the train and setting it on fire. Modi flew to the site.

Orders were given for the corpses to be brought to Ahmedabad in a convoy of trucks. The corpses were then displayed in the open on the hospital grounds, apparently for the purpose of postmortem examinations, as agitated crowds watched the grisly spectacle.

A retaliatory campaign of extermination by Hindu mobs against Muslims began hours later and lasted for more than two months, resulting in the death of more than 1,000 people and the displacement of 150,000. Women and girls were raped before being mutilated and set on fire. Homes, shops, restaurants, and mosques were looted and burned. The attackers, reportedly guided by computer printouts that listed the addresses of Muslim families, were on many occasions aided by the police or led by legislators in Modi's government. Many of the killers were identified as belonging to various Hindu right organizations. "Eighteen people from my family died," a survivor of the onslaught said, as quoted in *We Have No Orders to Save You*, a 2002 report from Human Rights Watch. "All the women died. My brother, my three sons, one girl, my wife's mother, they all died. My boys were aged ten, eight, and six. My girl was twelve years old. The bodies were piled up. I recognized them from parts of their clothes used for identification."

Even by the macabre standards of mass murder in India, there was something unusually disturbing about the Gujarat massacres. They had taken place in a relatively prosperous state, among people given to trade and business, rather than in a less-developed part of the country where a link might be made between deprivation and rage. But this connection in Gujarat, between economic prosperity and primal, sectarian violence, became one of the defining aspects of Modi's image, in India and among the diaspora, one reaffirming the other, the pride of wealth meeting the pride of identity.

In the aftermath of the massacres, Modi demonstrated not a shred of remorse or regret. In fact, he decided early on to turn questions about the massacres and his role in them into an attack on Gujarat, and on India, especially when the Bush administration decided, in 2005, to deny Modi a diplomatic visa and revoked his tourist/business visa for the "particularly severe violations of religious freedom" that had taken place under him.

In 2007, when asked by Karan Thapar, the host of a show on the Indian television channel CNN-IBN, "Why can't you say that you regret the killings that happened? Why can't you say maybe the government should have done more to protect Muslims?" Modi walked out of the interview. In 2013, as he was emerging as a prime ministerial candidate, Modi responded to a similar question with a convoluted analogy. "If someone else is driving, and we are sitting in the back seat, and even then if a small *kutte ka baccha* comes under the wheel, do we feel pain or not? We do." Reuters translated *kutte ka baccha* as "puppy," which, while technically accurate, missed the point: *Kutte ka baccha*, or "progeny of a dog," is an insult.

Modi also began to say that he had been given "a clean chit" about his role in the massacres by a team appointed by the Indian Supreme Court. His legions of supporters modified this statement, endlessly repeating that the Supreme Court had cleared him of any culpability in relation to the massacres. Jagdish Bhagwati and Arvind Panagariya, economists at Columbia University, wrote to *The Economist* asserting this, arguing that what the magazine had earlier called a "pogrom" was really a riot and that a quarter of those killed were Hindus. In some ways, this response is almost as disturbing as what happened during the massacres themselves. Modi's supporters were willing to ignore the question of responsibility for the sake of what they saw as the higher priority of a new India, now a superpower respected by the West. Large sections of the liberal Indian intelligentsia, writers and opinion makers, have chosen to remain silent. And then there are those who approve of Modi, knowing that he has been able to address all of new India's fantasies and fears in a way not achieved by any other comparable leader, taking it to great heights as an emerging capitalist power, asserting its place in the world, and unleashing its dark, nihilistic violence on marginalized people.

As for Modi's "clean chit," the devil is in the details. Modi, who is supposed to have been absolved by the Supreme Court, has never actually been tried by it. The Supreme Court was petitioned in 2008 by Citizens for Justice and Peace (CJP), an advocacy group seeking justice for the victims of the massacres. Led by Teesta Setalvad, a Gujarati activist, the CJP expressed its fear that the judicial process in Gujarat was compromised, in response to which the Supreme Court appointed a Special Investigation Team (SIT) to look into a select number of cases. In 2009, the court also asked the SIT to investigate a petition against Modi related to his involvement in the massacres, which was initiated by Zakia Jafri, whose husband, Ehsan Jafri, a Congress politician, was killed during them; she had previously approached the Gujarat Police and the Gujarat High Court, to no avail.

The SIT's final report in 2012 concluded that there was not enough evidence to prosecute Modi. But, as the journalist Hartosh Singh Bal (my close friend and former colleague) pointed out in *Open*, a current affairs magazine, those conclusions differed dramatically from the evidence in the report itself. One is left with the impression that the SIT was eager to find a lack of evidence no matter how much evidence actually existed. Maybe the SIT was right to be cautious. Bal was fired by *Open* just before the 2014 election for being too critical of the Hindu right; when Modi won, *Open* described his victory with the headline, "Triumph of the Will."

The SIT was also plagued by charges of interference from members seen as close to Modi and the Gujarat administration. Harish Salve, a senior lawyer appointed to guide the SIT as an *amicus curiae*, or "friend of the court," was removed for allegations of conflict of interest. He was also representing the Modi government in front of the Gujarat High Court in the matter of Ishrat Jahan, a nineteen-year-old Muslim college student who was killed by the police, who alleged she was a terrorist plotting to assassinate Modi. There had been other such extrajudicial executions in Gujarat, with more than thirty police officers and government ministers imprisoned for their involvement, all allegedly carried out under the direction of Amit Shah, the Gujarat minister of state during Modi's tenure and now the president of the BJP and home minister of India. A number of the police officers selected to join the SIT had allegedly been involved in these extrajudicial killings, as well as in the 2002 massacres. Salve's replacement, Raju Ramachandran, argued there was enough evidence to try Modi. He called for the cross-examination of Sanjiv Bhatt, a Gujarat police officer who had earlier stated that he was present at a meeting during which Modi directed the police to allow Hindus to vent their rage.

The overall tendency of Modi's government was, as Human Rights Watch described in its report, one of "subverting justice, protecting perpetrators, and intimidating those promoting accountability." Government officials seen as loyal to Modi, and under whose watch some of the worst killings took place, were rewarded with promotions and cushy posts. Those who provided evidence that raised questions about his role in the massacres found themselves subject to disciplinary measures, legal prosecution, threats, and scandals.

Three police officers who gave the National Commission for Minorities a transcript of a public speech delivered by Modi seven months after the massacres, in which he called camps set up for displaced Muslims "baby-producing centers," were summarily transferred. R. B. Sreekumar, a senior police officer who testified to a commission set up by the Gujarat government to investigate the train fire and the massacres, which was headed initially by a sole retired judge considered to be a Modi loyalist, was denied promotion and charged by the government with giving out "classified information." He had recorded a session during which a senior Modi official had coached him about how he should answer questions, including "tell[ing] the commission that no better steps could be taken" in terms of preventing the violence. Rahul Sharma, a police officer who gave the commission phone records allegedly proving that killers involved in the massacres had regularly been in touch with politicians and police officers, was charged by the Gujarat government with violating the state's Official Secrets Act. Haren Pandya, a minister in the Gujarat government who became a bitter rival of Modi's, and who testified in secret to an independent fact-finding panel about the riots, was murdered in March 2003, after he was publicly identified as a whistleblower and forced to resign his ministerial post. A dozen men, supposedly Islamist terrorists, were arrested for Pandya's murder; all of them were acquitted eight years later. Pandya's father maintained that Modi had orchestrated the killing.

In contrast, those who were indicted and sentenced to imprisonment for taking part in the massacres seemed to have a benevolent, gentle state looking out for their well-being. Maya Kodnani, an RSS member and BJP legislator, named by Modi as the Gujarat minister for women and child development in 2007, was in 2012 sentenced to twenty-eight years in prison for leading a mob that killed ninety-five people, including thirty-two women and thirty-three children. In 2014, she was let out on furlough due to poor health, and she has since been spotted taking selfies at a yoga retreat on the outskirts of Ahmedabad. Babu Bajrangi, a leader in the Bajrang Dal, a militant faction, who was also convicted for his role in the Gujarat massacres, told the investigative magazine *Tehelka* in 2007 that Modi was "a real man" who had changed judges on Bajrangi's behalf on a number of occasions to get him out of jail. Given a life sentence in 2012, Bajrangi is frequently out of prison on furlough, for reasons ranging from attending his niece's wedding to getting his eyes checked.

The circumstances, when laid down clearly, are so damning that it is astonishing that they can be airbrushed from Modi's record. But they show how, in Gujarat, Modi engineered a hybrid vigilante-police state, one in which the righteous were punished and perpetrators rewarded.

§

Modi ran Gujarat for more than a decade. The achievements he claims from this period depend on audience and situation, but they all emphasize his economic success, in particular the "double-digit growth rates" he engineered through what is known as "the Gujarat Model." The profile of Modi on the BJP website commends his "masterstroke of putting Gujarat on the global map" through an "ongoing campaign called the Vibrant Gujarat that truly transforms Gujarat into one of the most preferred investment destinations. The 2013 Vibrant Gujarat Summit drew participation from over 120 nations of the world, a commendable feat in itself."

Modi hired the US public relations firm APCO Worldwide to help promote the Vibrant Gujarat initiative, and in this too, he showed himself to be a truly modern Indian, concerned with his image among other nations of the world, particularly in the West. The West was a willing accomplice in Modi's ambitions, eager to turn the conversation away from sectarianism and death by mob violence and toward the business opportunities offered by the Gujarat model. In January 2015, the *Economist*, not particularly enamored of Modi, lauded his fiscal success in Gujarat, writing, "With just 5 percent of India's population and 6 percent of its land mass, [Gujarat] accounts for 7.6 percent of its GDP, almost a tenth of its workforce, and 22 percent of its exports." Loud expert voices, many of them in the diaspora, bolstered this triumphal narrative, including Vivek Dehejia, an economist at Carleton University in Ottawa; Bhagwati and Panagariya at Columbia; and Ashutosh Varshney, a political science professor at Brown. As the 2014 national elections drew nearer, they were joined in their support by more seemingly liberal figures, in India and abroad, who had in the past been associated with the Congress.

The truth about the Gujarat model was more complex. What had been achieved, in a state that was already more developed than many other parts of India, was a layer of infrastructure and globalized trade—roads, power, exports—topped off with a thick, treacly layer of hype. The state poverty figures under Modi remained unimpressive and employment levels stalled, while the quality of available jobs went down, with lower wages in both rural and urban areas compared to the national average. Almost half of Gujarat's children under the age of five were undernourished, in keeping with the shameful national average. (Panagariya, the Modi loyalist, argued that Indian children were stunted, even when compared to impoverished sub-Saharan African populations, not because of malnutrition, which was a "myth," but because of genetic limitations to their height.) The number of girls born in Gujarat compared to boys remains low, suggesting a continued bias for male children in a country known for its grotesquely patriarchal norms; and yet the state is in the forefront of providing surrogate mothers for wealthy Western populations.

Much was made of Modi's decision in 2008 to allow the Indian automobile manufacturer Tata to open a car factory in Gujarat, in particular after an attempt to do so in the traditionally left-leaning state of West Bengal had resulted in a violent farmers' uprising. Less was said, however, about the low-cost cars made at the Tata plant, which were in the habit of catching fire. As for the rhetoric about creating a new Singapore, Shanghai, or South Korea—Modi's metaphors of growth reveal a preference for authoritarian, homogeneous social systems—it has still remained rhetoric. A new city on the outskirts of Ahmedabad, constructed by architects brought in from Shanghai and touted, in 2012, as "the largest urbanization project in Indian history," turned out, three years later, as the *Wall Street Journal* reported, to consist of mostly empty office buildings.

In an Independence Day speech last August, Modi modified his "Make in India" slogan to a more contemporary "Startup India." But there was little about the wealth created under Modi that had to do with technological innovation. It depended instead on heedless resource extraction, crony capitalism, and competition for outsourcing work handed out by the West, all of which has been visible in India for decades. In Modi's case, this was exemplified by his closeness to the Gujarati billionaire Gautam Adani,* who had come swiftly to Modi's defense when the latter was criticized for the 2002 massacres. In November 2014, Adani accompanied Modi to the G-20 summit in Australia, a country in which he hoped to dig one of the largest, and most controversial, coal mines in the world. Although a series of international banks refused to fund the project, voicing concerns about its environmental impact, Adani nevertheless received a massive loan from the State Bank of India.

---

* By 2023, Adani would be one of the richest men in the world, at one point surpassing Jeff Bezos to be the second-richest person in the world.

The shortcomings of the Gujarat model are not particular to the state but to India as a whole. The difference is that Gujarat's supposed economic achievement helped distinguish Modi from other political leaders in India trying much the same things. So Gujarat was a success, even as India was something of a failure to the Indian elite supporting Modi—a paradox that was resolved by making him prime minister.

§

How, with the violent scandal and the political failure, to account for Modi's rise? The narrative of a growing India fed into it, stoked by the Indian elite and a Western media untrained to see nuances beyond the success of global capitalism in the aftermath of the Cold War. The outsourcing of Western IT and office services played into it, as did the granting of visas to Indians to work in the West. Even the rise of a security state targeting Muslims found deep echoes in the West. The killing of Muslims in Gujarat in 2002 came less than a year after the attacks of September 11, 2001, which meant that the old animosities of the Hindu right toward Muslims, Islam, and Pakistan found fertile ground in a United States whose wars abroad, first in Afghanistan and then in Iraq, featured the same enemies. India was an ally in the marketplace and in the war against Islamism, and it was a contrast to both the overly religious, anti-Western militancy that would consume Pakistan and the godless manipulators of market capitalism in China.

For many in the Indian diaspora, and for their upper-tier elite relatives back in India, the endless cover stories, op-ed articles, books, and films praising the new India—even as Islam, Muslims, and Pakistan were regularly criticized as failed systems incompatible with modernity—meant a kind of double bonus for their self-image, confirming their arrival as the white man's favorite kind of Indian. Thomas Friedman became a best-selling author and a hero to Indians with his account of rising India in *The World Is Flat*. It was a long way from Henry Kissinger's comments in the 1970s that Indians were "bastards" and that Indira Gandhi was a "bitch." All of this had been achieved not through Gandhian anti-colonialism or the mystical self-abnegation associated with India by the counterculture in 1960s America, but through the materialist terms acceptable in contemporary America: money, long hours, and power.

The model-minority status of the Indian diaspora in the United States was an uneasy one. It depended on an uncritical identification with the American ethos of success through work and competition, as well as with its counterpart, what Toni Morrison has called the "most enduring and efficient rite of passage into American culture: negative appraisals of the native-born black population." It meant attacks on the idea of the welfare state, of affirmative action, of impoverished and incarcerated minorities—a method transferable back home through Modi and the Hindu right's assault on minorities and the poor and contemporary India's valorization of wealth maximization and conspicuous consumption. But the truth remained that India was not America, and the gilded elite of the former toasted their lifestyles in a context of far greater poverty, surrounded by hundreds of millions of the dispossessed—potentially militant and far too great in numbers to be housed in the prisons and reservations favored by America. The status quo remained fragile, easily disrupted, and it required not just a party or a program—the BJP's rival, the Congress, favored the same kind of economics and national security state—but a strong man like Modi who could grasp the present in both fists, as he had done in Gujarat. The West, with its selective talk of human rights, was an uncertain ally in this respect, desirable for its power but also resented for its superior status. Its approval, suddenly granted, could also be taken away, denied as easily as the visa refused to Modi in 2005.

Modi, at the time, was planning to attend a US trade convention of Asian American hotel owners. With 700,000 Gujaratis living in the United States, probably the largest Indian group in the country, the State Department was well aware of the sensitivities involved. A press release about his visa denial noted "the great respect the United States has for the many successful Gujaratis who live and work in the United States and the thousands who are issued visas to the United States each month." Yet Gujarati support (and it is worth reiterating that some Gujaratis have resisted Modi's sectarian agenda at great cost to themselves) formed only one strand in his valorization among Indians of Hindu origin in the diaspora, regardless of their ethnicity. Indians from minority faiths (Muslims, Sikhs, and Christians) and those belonging to progressive groups kept a critical distance from Modi. These groups were instrumental in pressuring the United States into denying him a visa, and they later attempted to serve him with a legal summons for genocide during his triumphal visit to Madison Square Garden.

For many in the Indian diaspora, however, the denial of Modi's visa highlighted the double standards of the West, especially since the Bush administration was hardly a benign power when it came to Muslims. It also confirmed the diaspora's suspicion of liberal factions in America, the media, universities, and the human rights sector, which they believed were out to humiliate Indians and Hindus by pointing out their deficiencies. The most visceral manifestation of these attitudes came in the writings and talks produced by Rajiv Malhotra, an Indian based in New Jersey who fulminated against the conspiracy directed at Hindu India by Western academics in Western universities. Like Modi, he saw himself as a mouse manager taken for a snake charmer, a victim of those identified as enemies of Hindus by the RSS from its very inception—Muslims, leftists, and the West. Malhotra, described by the Indian journalist Shoaib Daniyal as the "Ayn Rand of internet Hindutva," was an early exponent of the inverted postcolonial doggerel common among Modi and his supporters. He spoke of the "Eurocentric framework" of Western academics writing about an "indigenous non-Western civilization," while he himself uttered breathtaking essentialisms about white women, Dalits (people belonging to India's most oppressed castes), African Americans, and "Abrahamic religions." Long influential among the Indian diaspora in the United States, Malhotra had to wait for Modi to become prime minister to achieve full respectability in India. But this New Jersey reincarnation of Ayn Rand, with his YouTube videos, Twitter feed, and enormously popular books (shadowed by accusations of plagiarism), was only the most obvious aspect of the entrepreneurial approach to the Hindu-right project as manifested by Indian Americans.

This approach, which involved think tanks, lobbies, social media, networking, and "nonpartisan" pressure groups, added a new, globalized dimension to the established cultish practices of the RSS and the mob politics of the BJP—something Modi grasped perfectly. He liked his Indian American experts for the global aura they gave him and for the way they burnished his reputation as the Indian icon of the new century, committed to running India in a way it had never been run before. So, while the Indian diaspora's main fixation in the United States was a kind of cultural war—attempts to change references to Hinduism in school textbooks, smear campaigns against Western scholars of Hinduism, and the introduction at universities of programs and chairs in Hinduism that would be taught by individuals with questionable scholarly credentials but possessing the vital attribute of belonging to the faith—in India it would focus on bringing about Modi's victory in the national elections.

Modi's electoral campaign, described as India's first "presidential" campaign, was carried out along American lines with the focus as much on Modi as on his party. Lance Price, a former BBC journalist turned spin doctor for Tony Blair, was brought in to write the story of the election; Andy Marino, an unknown British writer, was given full access to Modi for an atrociously written hagiography that defended him on everything, including the Gujarat massacres. The campaign also featured the direct imprint of the Indian American diaspora, including a purportedly nonpartisan group called Citizens for Accountable Governance (CAG).

With members drawn from the alumni of Columbia and Brown, and former employees of JP Morgan and Goldman Sachs, the CAG provided data analysis and slick marketing tools for the campaign, with holograms of Modi beamed, like some kind of Sith lord, into distant Indian villages.

Yet beneath the modern, entrepreneurial campaign, there remained the minority baiting, the majoritarian aggressiveness, the riots, the intimidation, and the abuse. Among the crowds in India, Modi, having first softened them up with populist language that stood in direct contradiction to his business-friendly ethos in the boardrooms and conference centers of the West, poured out his usual sectarian invective, referring to himself as a *sevak*—a religious devotee. In the eastern part of India, just days after more than thirty Muslims had been killed in Assam in riots targeting them for their supposed origins in neighboring Bangladesh*, Modi, hands full of theatrical gestures, voice punctuated by dramatic pauses, spoke of how after the elections and his victory, Bangladeshis in India would have to pack up their bags and leave.

It was done with expertise, with subtlety, and always with an awareness of the business-friendly image being promoted abroad.

---

* This story is pursued in greater detail in Chapter 4 of this book.

Amit Shah was put in charge of campaigning in the northern state of Uttar Pradesh, an important arena for the national elections. Three months after he took over, riots broke out between Hindus and Muslims, the majority of the dead and the displaced being Muslims. Shah made sure, in a subsequent speech in April 2014, to accuse Muslims of raping and killing Hindus and talked of the elections as an opportunity to teach a lesson to such perpetrators of evil. The Election Commission of India, which prohibits appealing to voters on sectarian grounds, briefly banned Shah from campaigning, but Modi's election drive proceeded without a hitch.

As Modi went about his business, wielding swords at rallies and berating "secularism," the word used in India to emphasize its constitutional principle of equal rights for all religious beliefs, his devotees in India and the United States went about their mob business on the internet and in the media and social media. There was the innovative abuse directed at the 69 percent who would not vote for him, who did not buy into his vision—the more polite terms being "presstitute," "sickularist," and "libtard." The new Indians boasted of Modi, of his manly 56-inch chest (it's actually 44 inches, his waist 41, and his belly 45, if his personal tailor is to be believed), but inches were only another way of expressing Modi's machismo. Teenagers tattooed images of Modi on their bodies, and he was lauded as the country's most eligible bachelor. The fact that he was in fact married, to a woman with whom he had never lived, who has never been given financial support—and who, after Modi became prime minister, would be denied a passport because she possessed no marriage certificate—was largely forgotten, or drowned out with abuse and threats.

§

In an essay a few months after the Gujarat massacres, Ashis Nandy, a clinical psychologist and one of India's best-known public intellectuals, recalled how he had interviewed Modi in the early '90s, when he was "a nobody, a small-time RSS *pracharak* trying to make it as a small-time BJP functionary." Nandy wrote, "It was a long, rambling interview, but it left me in no doubt that here was a classic, clinical case of a fascist. I never use the term 'fascist' as a term of abuse; to me it is a diagnostic category." Modi, Nandy wrote,

> met virtually all the criteria that psychiatrists, psycho-analysts, and psychologists had set up after years of empirical work on the authoritarian personality. He had the same mix of puritanical rigidity, narrowing of emotional life, massive use of the ego defense of projection, denial, and fear of his own passions combined with fantasies of violence—all set within the matrix of clear paranoid and obsessive personality traits. I still remember the cool, measured tone in which he elaborated a theory of cosmic conspiracy against India that painted every Muslim as a suspected traitor and a potential terrorist.

Nandy soon found himself the subject of a criminal case lodged by the Gujarat Police. It accused him, of all things, of disturbing the harmonious relationship between religious communities. In a way, it proved Nandy's point about the authoritarian personality who attempts to silence all dissent while expressing no doubts at all about his own actions and beliefs. Vinod Jose, in a meticulously researched profile published in 2012 in *Caravan* magazine (I am a contributing editor to *Caravan*), had noted how Modi made others apologize, turning criticism into entrepreneurial opportunity. In February 2003, two Indian industrialists, at an event with

Modi, commented on the Gujarat violence; Modi engineered a written apology from the Confederation of Indian Industry (CII), the trade association that had organized the event. "We, in the CII, are very sorry for the hurt and pain you have felt," the letter stated, adding that it regretted "very much the misunderstanding that has developed since the sixth of February, the day of our meeting in New Delhi."

For those who have not apologized, and who have continued to stand up to Modi, different measures have been applied: legal intimidation, government pressure, social abuse, scurrilous gossip, police cases, and mob violence. Setalvad, one of Modi's staunchest opponents, found her residence in Mumbai raided last July by the Central Bureau of Investigation, a federal agency, even as the Gujarat government attempted to have her arrested for financial fraud.* The Ford Foundation, which has funded some of the projects carried out by Setalvad's organization, discovered itself in the crosshairs of both the federal government and the state of Gujarat, the latter accusing the foundation, in a repeat of the charges against Nandy, of "abetting communal disharmony."

With a defeat in November's state elections for Bihar, in the eastern part of the country, Modi's new India has amped up its sectarian Hindu nationalism, unleashing an astonishing degree of violence against all those who might not subscribe to this worldview, training its rhetoric and weaponry against anyone who might be identified as "anti-national," which includes all those critical of Modi, the Hindu right, and Indian nationalism. In January 2015,

---

* Setalvad remains constantly in and out of prison. The BBC called her "perhaps India's most hounded activist," her bank accounts frozen, her house and office raided, and subject to threats and vilification in the press and on social media. "The Gujarat authorities have been hounding Setalvad for nearly two decades, filing a slew of false charges, many of which remain pending, manipulating the criminal justice system as a threat," Human Rights Watch said in a report in 2022.

immigration officials prevented a Greenpeace India staffer from boarding a flight to London, where she was scheduled to speak to British members of parliament about the environmental risk of a proposed mine in Madhya Pradesh, in central India, co-owned by a company listed on the London stock exchange. The government also identified Greenpeace India as working against the national interest, canceling its license to receive funds from outside India. Later that year, the writer Arundhati Roy was issued a criminal contempt notice by a Nagpur court, for an article she published in *Outlook* magazine about G. N. Saibaba, a disabled political dissident confined to a wheelchair, who had been awaiting trial for a year. Roy argued Saibaba should not be prevented from getting bail if Bajrangi and Kodnani, convicted for their role in the 2002 massacres, could, and if Amit Shah, once charged with ordering extrajudicial executions, functioned with impunity as president of the BJP "and the right-hand man of Prime Minister Narendra Modi."

Shortly afterward, Rohith Vemula, a twenty-six-year-old PhD student at the University of Hyderabad who was a Dalit, the most oppressed of India's castes, committed suicide. Vemula had protested the BJP student wing's forcible disruption of the screening of a documentary on riots provoked by the BJP as part of Modi's prime ministerial campaign, and had been targeted by the Hindu right. Described as anti-national by two ministers in Modi's cabinet, and barred by authorities at the University of Hyderabad from entering its hostels and public spaces, a practice reminiscent of the ostracization of Dalits by upper-caste Hindus, he hanged himself.

In February, Kanhaiya Kumar, a student leader at Jawaharlal Nehru University, a public university in Delhi portrayed as an elite left bastion by the Hindu right, was arrested by the Delhi Police on the orders of a BJP minister for sedition. During two of Kumar's court appearances, lawyers (or men who claimed to be lawyers) assaulted students and faculty who had come to show their solidarity with Kumar. For good measure, they also beat up journalists who attempted to record the violence.

As in the 2002 massacres and their aftermath, the degree of violence under Modi's rule differs depending on the target. In the case of Mohammad Akhlaq, a Muslim man lynched in September on the suspicion of eating beef, it was a mob at the door with swords and pistols. When a group of writers returned the national awards they had received in protest of the Modi government's sectarianism, a Bollywood actor led a march against these writers for having "hurt the spirit of India," ending with a much-publicized meeting with Modi.

Against this backdrop, with violence piling up almost faster than can be recorded, Modi has functioned as a talking mask. Despite his ubiquity on social media, with two Twitter feeds, one personal and one official, and despite being constantly photographed in expensive clothes—he wore a reportedly $16,000 suit made on Savile Row when meeting Obama in Delhi last January, a gift to him from a businessman, which was auctioned off later—he is perhaps the most closed-off head of state India has seen. He rarely gives interviews to the media, and never to journalists who might be critical of him. But he is always making pronouncements, sometimes providing free internet for rural India with the assistance of Mark Zuckerberg, sometimes solving climate change for the world in a Twitter conversation with @potus, tweeting an endless stream of banalities.

His performance is a banal kind of greatness, calibrated finely over a decade, even as behind and around him violence moves in ranks that make it hard to tell the difference between the mob and the police. Yet the authoritarian personality of Modi would be without impact, without significance, if it did not resonate with the millions of authoritarian personalities among the professionalized classes in India and the diaspora, in Silicon Valley, and New Jersey, and Mumbai, and Delhi, among those who have risen so suddenly as to be suffering from vertigo, who feel liberated from all meaningful knowledge, whether from the past or the present, and who feel enslaved by their liberation. While they harness their souls to the standards of professional, material, Westernized success, to the air conditioning that Modi mocks when on the campaign trail, their insecurity and humiliation about the West makes them extract sustenance from Modi's utterances about Hindus having invented plastic surgery.

Modi cannot be held solely responsible for such rage and despair, even if he amplifies it. His supporters, at home and in the West, the West itself, which chooses to ignore the violence in India, and a complaisant liberal intelligentsia, concerned more with its career prospects than with standing up to Modi, have to share the responsibility. There is also much continuity between Modi's India and what preceded it, including the way in which the Congress stood aside during the 2002 massacres and their aftermath, selectively exploiting the culpability of Modi and his government but never genuinely interested in justice; nurturing Hindu majoritarianism under the guise of nationalism; promoting the enrichment of a select few.

From this hollowed-out form of success, bereft of love, spirituality, and justice, meaning can only emerge from banality and hatred. Modi's contradictions and lies channel the confusions of his supporters perfectly. In a manner reminiscent of the vanguards of China's Cultural Revolution or the nativists flocking to Donald Trump, they accuse the old elites of holding back the nation and the culture from true greatness. They attack those responsible for the ruined past, the uncertain future, and the endless present. They assail the "anti-nationals" who stand in their way, beating and molesting people while shouting, "*Bharat Mata Ki Jai!*" They demand people say it to prove they are not traitors, emboldened by a meeting of the BJP in March, led by Modi, that declared a refusal to use the slogan as tantamount to disrespecting the Indian constitution. They hammer, with swords and guns and smartphones and double-digit growth, at the doors of the beef-eaters, the environmentalists, the university students, the feminists, the Dalits, the leftists, the dissenting writers, the skeptics, the "anti-nationals"— anyone who will not declare, both fists clenched, *"Bharat Mata Ki Jai!"* They have a rage that must burn itself out, and all that stands between them and the ashes of their rage is the astonishing, amazing phenomenon of a world that can still produce, from the crushed bottom layers of Indian society, people who, with every bit of the dignity and courage they can muster, resist the lure of their silent, lonely, aloof, admired, and unloved leader.

Chapter 2
An Alien Visitation

The Worst Industrial Disaster in the History of the World

> A caption: some kind of meteorite or alien visitation has led to the creation of a miracle: the Zone. Troops were sent in and never returned. It was surrounded by barbed wire and a police cordon.
>
> —Geoff Dyer, *Zona*

The ruins of the Union Carbide pesticide factory lie in the very center of India, in the state of Madhya Pradesh, which means "Middle State."* There, in the capital city of Bhopal, inside the old city that sits across a lake from the new city, inside the crumbling but imposing fortress gates and beyond the twisting medieval alleyways and public squares, past makeshift shacks, scrubland, and slime-filled canals, surrounded by a boundary wall and guarded by a contingent of policemen, is the site of the worst industrial disaster in the history of the world. But for all that, the factory is not inaccessible. It can be visited, with the correct permit. The walls surrounding it are full of breaches. There are slums right outside the factory site, from which children sneak in to play cricket.

---

* First published in *The Baffler*, no. 26, October 2014.

Cattle wander in to graze, making their way around discarded white sacks of pesticide, twisted pipes, and rusting metal parts. The blackened towers are visible from a distance.

There was a proposal, once, to turn the site into something else, into a national park that would include a memorial, a tourist center, a "craft village," a technology park, and an amusement park. But three decades have passed since the disaster that began late at night on December 2, 1984, and the guarded, abandoned factory site is just that: a guarded (but regularly breached), abandoned site, a place where anything could have happened and maybe did happen.

For the people of Old Bhopal who woke up on the night of December 2 finding it difficult to breathe, their eyes burning, it was as if some great, unknown evil had taken place. They did not think of the factory as the source of their distress, not unless they had worked there and knew of its troubles or had been among those active in protesting its location in their midst. Most people thought there was a fire in a chili warehouse somewhere, sending clouds of toxic fumes their way—and because burning chilies are sometimes used to chase off evil spirits, this seemed to be a case of an exorcism gone out of control, the protecting magic indistinguishable from the possessing evil.

But the source of this particular evil was, in fact, the factory. An accident there had sent forty metric tons of methyl isocyanate (MIC), a lethal chemical, into a runaway reaction that released a toxic gas. The gas filled the night air of Old Bhopal and entered into people's bloodstreams, where it then dissolved into hydrocyanic acid, attacking the lungs, respiratory tracts, kidneys, liver, and brain. In order to get away from the choking, burning air, people abandoned their houses and tenements. They ran away from the slums, out of Old Bhopal, across the lake and the hills that divide New Bhopal from Old Bhopal and that would keep the city's wealthier residents relatively safe even as the poor choked on the fumes. They poured into the new city, into the railway station, some dying in the stampede, others succumbing to the fumes. So many people died that mass cremations and burials took place, bodies piled one on top of another. Corpses were loaded onto trucks and hastily driven out of the city.

It is possible to say, in the case of the 1986 Chernobyl disaster, that three people died immediately at the site of the explosions and that twenty-eight more died from acute radiation syndrome within the year. It is also possible to say, with regard to the accident at Fukushima in 2011, that so far there have been no radiation-related deaths. But it is not possible to say, in spite of all those corpses and the many years that have passed, exactly how many people died in Bhopal from the MIC leak. The Indian government initially claimed extremely modest figures for deaths and injuries, but there are estimates, based partly on the number of funeral shrouds sold the day after the accident, that at least 3,000 people died within the first twenty-four hours. After that, the assessment of fatalities fluctuates wildly, but it's likely that more than 20,000 people have died in the past thirty years from effects of the gas.*

The fallout of the leak extends well beyond even that, with perhaps half a million survivors impaired with breathing difficulties, vision problems, spells of unconsciousness, and psychological disorders. Women suffer a high rate of miscarriages, and children

---

* The usual range quoted is 3,000 to 4,000 within the first twenty-four hours; I have cited the lower end. According to Amnesty International, 7,000 people died "within days," a total that climbed to 22,000 in the following years, with another 100,000 people subject to "chronic and debilitating illnesses." The Bhopal Memorial Hospital and Research Centre, run by a trust established in the aftermath of the accident, estimates that 500,000 people suffered "agonizing injuries." A report in the *Guardian* noted that the office of Bhopal's medical commissioner "registered 22,149 directly related deaths up to December 1999."

are prone to birth defects. The abandoned factory overruns its boundary walls even if it appears to be sequestered; chemicals stored on site or dumped into pits seep into the groundwater and make their way into the tube wells and taps of surrounding slums. Today, thirty years after the events of December 2 and 3, 1984, the factory continues to pulsate with its evil magic.

Safety Last

Union Carbide, founded in 1917 and since 2001 a wholly owned subsidiary of the Dow Chemical Company, set up its Bhopal factory in 1969. But it had established its presence in India long before then. Although the Indian economy was driven at the time by autarkic principles that limited foreign control of Indian companies, Union Carbide had found a way of operating freely and profitably within such notional restrictions. Like Nestlé and Unilever, other giant multinationals, it concentrated on the kinds of things needed by a developing country, packed its board of directors and senior management with Indian industrialists and the relatives of important politicians, and emphasized its own, somewhat spurious, Indianness.*

In reality, it was one of the largest chemical companies in the United States, with corporate headquarters in New York (later moved to Danbury, Connecticut) and an Asia head office in Hong Kong. The 50.9 percent stock it held in Union Carbide India Limited (UCIL), its Indian subsidiary, was a controlling stake, and senior positions at UCIL were filled on instructions from Hong Kong or New York. Although UCIL's most profitable group was the battery division, with a virtual monopoly in India, the factory in Bhopal was set up to manufacture a product aimed at farmers rather than urban households. This was the pesticide carbaryl,

---

* Unilever, an Anglo-Dutch company, has its own toxic history in India; in 2001 it was caught dumping mercury in Kodaikanal, Tamil Nadu.

marketed under the brand name Sevin. Another pesticide, Temik, was also made at the factory, in smaller quantities, but Union Carbide's promise of food for the masses was carried largely by Sevin, a white powder sold in paper bags of twenty-five kilos each.

Sevin came from an industry with a macabre past. Pesticides originated in chemical weapons, and German firms, with their expertise in poisoning British and French soldiers during World War I, dominated the business in the beginning. One such firm was BASF, part of World War II's notorious IG Farben group; the group ran a unit called IG Auschwitz and produced Zyklon B, a gas pumped into the chambers at the death camps.* Two decades later, the Dow Chemical Company manufactured napalm so that the Vietnamese could be killed cheaply and easily in large numbers. And agricultural pesticides themselves had unintended consequences. Rachel Carson's book *Silent Spring*, published in 1962, showed how DDT, at the time a popular pesticide—and one still widely used in India—is a nonbiodegradable toxin that remains present in fish and wildlife and even works its way into human breast milk.

Maybe this history has little to do with the coming of Union Carbide to Bhopal. No doubt, there was some Indian demand for pesticides, which, along with chemical fertilizers, were considered to be the key ingredients in India's so-called Green Revolution, allowing food production to keep pace with a growing population. That technology has since been called into question as unsafe and unsustainable for both the land and the people who farm it, but the Indian government in the sixties would have had few doubts about the seemingly advanced Western science represented by Sevin.

Union Carbide, in any case, promoted Sevin as a safer alternative to DDT: less dangerous for humans, biodegradable, and

---

* BASF is still in business and is a leading union-buster; in the 1980s, protests over conditions at one of its US plants (in Louisiana's "cancer alley") ended in a five-year lockout.

effective against a wide range of pests. It did not publicize the fact that its process for manufacturing Sevin required a number of lethal chemicals, including phosgene (one of the gases used during the trench warfare of World War I, along with mustard gas and chlorine) and MIC.* Made by combining phosgene and monomethylamine, MIC is a highly volatile chemical; it reacts with water and other substances and needs to be kept cool to prevent unwanted reactions. The only other Union Carbide factory that produced MIC was located in Institute, West Virginia—most chemical companies avoided MIC and preferred a different, more expensive, way of producing pesticides similar to Sevin—and Institute had had its share of accidents, especially leaks in the MIC unit.

The Bhopal factory started small, with a "formulation" unit that mixed already prepared chemicals to produce Sevin. The mixing procedure was fairly basic, and there were many such formulation factories in India. But the idea, from the very beginning, had been for Union Carbide to create a "technical" unit, one in which advanced proprietary technologies would be used to manufacture the pesticides from scratch. The Indian government, according to Union Carbide, wanted the technology to be imported into the country, which is probably true. Government leaders would have seen it as a step toward becoming a developed economy, boosting

---

* The poem "Dulce et Decorum est" by Wilfred Owen describes a World War I poison gas attack: "Gas! Gas! Quick, boys!—an ecstasy of fumbling, / Fitting the clumsy helmets just in time; / But someone still was yelling out and stumbling, / And flound'ring like a man in fire or lime … / Dim, through the misty panes and thick green light, / As under a green sea, I saw him drowning." A woman I met in 2004 named Ghazala, who was twelve at the time of the Bhopal disaster and was blinded by it, described her experience of the fumes to me in a metaphor that was the obverse of Owen's, of feeling "like a fish out of water." But the experience, in essence, was the same—that of being unable to breathe and of being trapped in a deadly, alien environment.

both agriculture and industry. Union Carbide, too, was interested in manufacturing locally. It had been exporting Sevin to India for some years; now it could eliminate international shipping expenses, take advantage of lower labor costs, and be centrally located in a market it perceived as the largest in the world after China, with 550 million acres under cultivation and a population of 560 million.

After initially importing MIC directly from the West Virginia factory, the Bhopal factory installed its own MIC unit in 1979. The completed setup, in anticipation of heavy demand for Sevin, had an annual production capacity of 5,000 metric tons. But the market for Sevin turned out to be far smaller than expected, with Indian farmers unable to afford it and preferring indigenous products, and so, through the early 1980s, the Bhopal factory operated at half its production capacity.

The Contamination of Everything

There had always been shortcuts in safety procedures.* Union Carbide built the factory in a densely populated urban area over protests from local people and legislators, and it chose to store large

---

* According to researcher Bridget Hanna, the Bhopal factory was, from the beginning, less safe than the factory Union Carbide operated in West Virginia. In her article "Bhopal: Unending Disaster, Enduring Resistance," Hanna writes: "Although UCC claims that its plant in Bhopal was built to the same safety specifications as its American facilities, when it was finally constructed there were at least eleven significant differences in safety and maintenance policies between the Bhopal factory and its sister facility in Institute, West Virginia. For example, the West Virginia plant had an emergency plan, computer monitoring, and used inert chloroform for cooling their MIC tanks. Bhopal had no emergency plan, no computer monitoring, and used brine, a substance that may dangerously react with MIC, for its cooling system. The Union Carbide Karamchari Sangh (Workers' Union), a union of Bhopal workers that formed in the early 1980s, recognized the dangers at the factory but their agitation for safer conditions produced no changes."

quantities of MIC there even though electricity in the area was undependable and temperatures regularly crossed 110 Fahrenheit in the summer. When there were mechanical failures, as in the alpha-naphthol unit, the company directed poorly paid contract workers to crush the alpha-naphthol with hammers and carry it to the reactor; the workers were unaware throughout of their exposure to toxic vapors. And once the market failed to match production capacity, other safety measures were eliminated, seemingly to save costs in a factory that was nowhere as profitable as had been originally envisioned.

An inspection team visiting from the United States in 1982 noted several safety problems, and one of the visiting inspectors sent a telex stating that they "had to destroy 1.8 MT [metric tons] of MIC due to water contamination/trimerization." A supervisor and one of the operators got injured the same year during a chemical spill. Some of the technicians skilled in chemistry, hearing rumors that the factory would be closed down, left for other jobs; a number of them went to Iraq, then fighting a war with Iran. Management staff began leaving too, replaced by people from UCIL's profitable and influential battery division, who, it was said, had little knowledge of pesticide factories. By 1983 the World Agricultural Business Team at Union Carbide's headquarters in New York had decided to sell the Bhopal factory. If the company was unable to dispose of it by the end of the next fiscal year, the factory would be closed down and the costs written off.

This meant that most of the safety devices at the factory, especially those intended to contain MIC, were inoperative by the time of the disaster. The production of MIC had halted, but large amounts of the chemical were stored in three underground tanks. The cooling system, which could slow down unexpected reactions, had been shut off to cut costs; the scrubber unit that neutralized escaping chemicals wasn't functioning; the flare tower at the very top, meant to burn off toxic vapors if all else failed, had been dismantled for repairs. All that was left was a wind sock, which allowed the workers on the night of the disaster to see the direction of the wind, heading southeast toward the crowded, poor quarters of Chola, J.P. Nagar, and the railway station.

Some of this can still be seen when one visits the factory, as I did ten years ago. Time seems half-suspended, the night of the accident preserved in the fashion of some permanently stopped Hiroshima clock. The factory sprawls on its sixty-two-acre grounds, the blackened pipes and rusting metal parts evoking something that could be either the remnants of a nineteenth-century industrialism or an utterly alien technology. The shelves and racks in the quality control building still hold bottles of chemicals, the labels faded and covered in thick layers of dust. There are broken, small-scale models of the alpha-naphthol, MIC, and Sevin units in the control room, eerie echoes of the looming structures visible through the dense vegetation.

At the Sevin unit, light reflects off the silver gleam of strings of mercury drops, and the blackish-brown dirt around a collapsed chute has a thick, sweet, chemical odor with just a hint of putrefying animal flesh. In the MIC unit, lengths of a black hose are visible, perhaps left over from the night of the accident, when a hose was apparently used to flush out solid impurities choking a set of pipes. The washing was a routine operation, and the water should have come out through some vents; instead, it was blocked by the impurities and flowed in the direction of 610, one of three underground tanks used to store MIC. When water entered 610, it reacted with the MIC, building up a flow of gases that retraced the route to the MIC unit. With the cooling system shut down, the reaction in 610 was fast, and without the scrubber and flare tower, the journey of the gases was unimpeded.

The tank itself, a giant black cylinder with a spout, lies on the ground, long removed from its underground housing. Around it, it can sometimes seem as if a cycle of renewal is in progress: creepers and shrubs making their way back into the buildings; red, orange, and purple bursts of flowers; bird eggs in the rubble of the administrative office; perhaps a snake lurking near the formulation shed. But the flowers and snakes exist not in paradise but in a modern wasteland, where the sheds contain sacks and drums stuffed with Sevin and naphthol residue. Along the northern wall, next to the slum of Atal-Ayub Nagar, there are piles of rubbish, with white Sevin sacks strewn on the ground. In the concrete tanks where liquid waste was dumped, a dark crust has formed on the surface, shot through with yellow streaks like frozen fat in a meat curry.

The damage, of course, extends well beyond the boundary walls. Samples tested separately by Greenpeace, the Boston-based Citizens' Environmental Laboratory, and the People's Science Institute, an independent Indian organization, have shown the presence of toxins in the drinking water of nearby slums, and farmland in the area remains unusable.

The Butcher's Bill

Those affected by the poisons make do the best they can. Protesters have caused the water pumps in slums like Atal-Ayub Nagar to be painted red and marked as dangerous. Municipal tankers deliver water at irregular intervals to a few black plastic drums placed in the slums by the government. There is a hospital for the afflicted, an expensive auto-rickshaw ride away from the old city, and a cheap, shabby housing estate known as the Gas Widows' Rehabilitation Colony. Within this grudging setup, people go on: the woman with the twisted limbs, the man who lost his family, the boy who turned schizophrenic, the girl with the unusually large head. For those who are part of the dwindling original group affected directly by the MIC leak, their accounts are composed of memory fragments and body parts, yellowed paper and shabby surroundings, eagerness and hopelessness.

If there is any sustenance, it is provided by the victims themselves and the two local activist organizations that have struggled in their cause. In the immediate aftermath of the accident, concerned citizens and activist groups banded together in a loose coalition called the Morcha to provide help to the afflicted. When the Morcha broke up, two principal organizations emerged, the Bhopal Gas Peedit Mahila Udyog Sangathan, led by Abdul Jabbar*, and the Bhopal Group for Information and Action, run by Satinath Sarangi. Without these two organizations, the first a feisty trade-union-style outfit with deep local roots, the other excellent at disseminating information on the internet and liaising with foreign activists and groups, the victims would have been entirely at the mercy of the Indian government and Union Carbide.

The government quickly declared all the victims "wards" of the Indian state. This was done, it was said, to protect them from the predatory American lawyers hanging around Bhopal, asking people to place their thumbprints on documents in exchange for promises of compensation money. In hindsight, it's hard not to think they might have been better off as clients of those pinstriped hucksters than as neglected wards of a callous state.

The Indian government, unilaterally representing the victims in its suit against Union Carbide, tried to have a trial in the United States, where there were no upper limits to compensation. Union Carbide asked for the case to be heard in India, pleading the excellence of Indian courts. It won the argument, and the case went to trial in India, where in 1989, five years after the accident,

---

* Jabbar eventually became a friend, someone I visited over the years. Principled, poor, and feisty to the end, Jabbar died in 2019, at the age of 61.

the government decided to accept an out-of-court settlement of $470 million in compensation from Union Carbide. For Union Carbide, and for the Dow Chemical Company, which later acquired Union Carbide, this settled the matter in perpetuity.

Dow has insisted that it has no connection to Bhopal at all, a position that has not, however, stopped it from buying up the domain bhopal.com to present its one-sided story. It insists that the average victim should have received $500, which, as one of its PR flacks argued in 2002, is "plenty good for an Indian."* The Indian government distributed that plenty-good money at a glacial pace, claiming in 2006 that it had finally finished the payouts.

But the leak also prompted a criminal case, and that case has yet to be resolved. Union Carbide, which at first described MIC as no more dangerous than tear gas, began its search for a scapegoat by blaming Sikh terrorists (there was a Sikh secessionist movement in India at the time). It then changed course to argue, based on a study authored by an Indian engineer working for the management firm Arthur D. Little, that the factory was sabotaged by an unidentified, disgruntled worker. This study was based on the argument that there is a "reflexive tendency" among workers to lie, on the year-old testimony of a single engineer at the factory, and on a statement by a twelve-year-old canteen boy that the workers had looked tense that night.

---

* Two years later, Dow representatives stated in a press release that they "wishe[d] to retract" the remark, the "poor phrasing" of which had "often come back to haunt" them. In the same release, Dow made it clear that while it has no plan to offer reparations to the Bhopal victims and "cannot and will not take responsibility" for the disaster (because "Dow's sole and unique responsibility is to its shareholders"), a different public relations strategy is in place when it comes to its dealings with Americans. Dow "settled Union Carbide's asbestos liabilities in the U.S." and "paid U.S. $10 million to one family poisoned by a Dow pesticide," according to the statement. "This is a mark of Dow's corporate responsibility."

In India, the Central Bureau of Investigation (CBI) took charge of the factory after the accident, considering it material evidence in the ongoing criminal case. But the legal ownership of the factory is another matter. In 1991 the Indian Supreme Court, reviewing the original settlement of 1989, upheld the compensation amount of $470 million, although it struck down the clause guaranteeing Union Carbide and UCIL immunity from criminal proceedings. In 1992 Union Carbide announced that it would sell its 50.9 percent stake in UCIL and put $17 million of the proceeds into a trust aimed at building a hospital for accident survivors. A few days after this announcement, the chief judicial magistrate of Bhopal ordered the confiscation of the company's remaining assets in India. In April 1994 the Supreme Court allowed Union Carbide to go ahead with the sale, and in November of that year the majority stake in UCIL was bought up by McLeod Russel India Limited, an Indian company owned by the B.M. Khaitan group. The Bhopal factory, in effect, belonged to the new owners, although it was technically still in possession of the CBI and the state government.

What all this corporate maneuvering really means is impossible to tell. In October 1997, when the Madhya Pradesh Pollution Control Board commissioned a report on toxins at the site, the factory still belonged to McLeod Russel (which had, since acquiring UCIL, changed the name to Eveready Industries India Limited). But in July 1998 EIIL turned over the lease to the government of Madhya Pradesh. The site remains, according to most accounts, contaminated.

Meanwhile, in spite of his professed faith in the excellence of Indian law, Union Carbide CEO Warren Anderson, who had flown to Bhopal after the accident, decided not to stay around for the criminal trial. A brief arrest, a bail of $2,000, and he was back in the United States, where he now lives a retired life in the Hamptons, playing golf. His status as a wanted man in India amounts to nothing, although Greenpeace activists or foreign journalists sometimes show up at his doorstep and try to elicit a response to the disaster.

Anderson isn't Eichmann. In "Hunting Warren Anderson," an investigative segment directed by John Firth and aired on Australia's SBS TV, Anderson looks like just another aging corporate official. When the crew traces him to his house, he is merely a shadow glimpsed through a window, a tall man, perhaps leaning over a kitchen counter. Anderson doesn't come out of the house in the film. Instead, it's Mrs. Anderson who does the talking, an elderly woman at the wheel of a large car. They have a family party later that night, and it is uncatered. Her voice quivers in outrage as she tells the reporters standing in her driveway, "Get off his back."*

Come Back Now, Dow

Mrs. Anderson's outrage is shared by many members of the Indian elite, who seem to feel that this business of talking about the dead and dying of Bhopal has gone on for far too long. The first decade of Indian response was marked by the state's great indifference toward the victims and even complicity with Union Carbide and its successors. That has now given way to the attitude among the upper classes that the victims and their supporters are holding back India's inexorable progress. Basking in the profitable embrace of neoliberalism, the elite that loves to love US corporations and loves to hate its poor has made significant efforts to make sure that Dow feels welcome and fully at home in India.

Led by Dow partners such as the tycoon Ratan Tata, a group of Indian industrialists, many of them luminaries of something

---

* Anderson died in 2014, at the age of 92, his retirement activities apparently consisting of gardening, fishing, and baking bread. See https://thebaffler.com/latest/death-enemy-warren-anderson-1920-2014

called the India-US CEO Forum, offered in 2007 to clean up the Bhopal factory if only the government would agree to let Dow operate in India without "legal liability." This was meant to be a small footnote to the US-India Civil Nuclear Agreement, but the Indian government, after a public outcry, eventually backed off from providing legal cover. Dow's Indian dealings, meanwhile, remain mired in scandals, including bribes paid to Indian officials. In 2008, protesters successfully blocked construction of a Dow R&D plant in Chakan, near Mumbai.

But the machinations of Dow and its Indian compradors are part of a larger story. In India these days, there are fantasies of a hundred more Bhopals in the form of secrecy-shrouded nuclear plants and river-damming projects, of pharaonic, Ozymandian monuments rising from the valleys and the mountains. Against this, there are the small acts of resistance by a multitude that understands what the elites repeatedly get wrong: the evil of technologies meant to bring profits and power only to a few.

In front of the J.P. Nagar slum, there is a sculpture by the Dutch artist and Holocaust survivor Ruth Waterman. It has its back to the factory and faces the slum, a statue of a mother and a child made of plain concrete and raised on a small plinth, hastily erected while slum dwellers held back the baton-wielding policemen sent in to prevent it from going up. On the wall of the slum, talking back to the statue, is a scrawled slogan, black on plain brick, that says, "Hang Anderson."

But truth be told, no one really wants to, should they get the chance, place a noose around the neck of a former CEO. The Anderson they want to hang is Union Carbide, Dow, the Indian government, the India-US CEO Forum. The Anderson they want to hang is Ravana, the demon king sent up in flames when the festival of Navratri culminates in Dussehra. The Anderson they want to hang is the djinn who wafted across the rooftops of Bhopal that night, shrouded in toxic smoke. The Anderson they want to hang is Uncle Sam, the imperialist and plutocrat in his striped trousers and top hat. The Anderson they want to hang is an evil thing, a meteorite, an alien visitation.

Chapter 3
Nowhere Land

The Lost Dissidents of Manipur

Last winter I traveled to Moreh, a small town on the border between India and Burma*. Moreh sits at the very end of National Highway 39, an outpost of tin-roofed houses and small shops set amid palm trees and dirt tracks that appears quiet even during the day. The principal landmark is the police station, a dark run-down building that the policemen reserve for prisoners and weapons while they conduct their business from a gazebo on the front lawn. The main avenue wanders past the police station and ends, after a walk of twenty minutes, at a border checkpoint marked by a bamboo barrier and a pair of limp flags. Dusk comes early to this eastern edge of India, and since there is rarely any electricity, Moreh is ready for bed by the time the policemen go around to announce the evening curfew, blowing their whistles and tapping their sticks on the shop shutters, asking the odd drunkard who might be loitering on the streets to go home.

---

* First published in *Harper's Magazine*, January 2009. Burma is officially known as Myanmar, but I use the name preferred by the pro-democracy activists I met in my reporting, people who saw Myanmar as an imposition by the military regime.

The sleepiness of Moreh is deceptive. The border, crossed in daylight hours by local traders, opens onto Burma, an insular country that seems cut off from the world by its authoritarian government and the punitive sanctions of the United States and the European Union. And then there is Moreh itself, which is located in Manipur, a small, impoverished, and violent state in India's remote northeastern territories, more than a thousand miles from Delhi, a state that is largely off-limits to foreigners and visited by few Indians. Moreh is where India ends, which is to say that most of what one associates with India has disappeared long before one reaches this town, giving way instead to a reality that is substantially different from the official narratives produced in Delhi.

Two months before I made my trip, there had been an unusually large number of references to the border in the Indian press. A series of demonstrations had broken out in Burma, led by Buddhist monks with upturned begging bowls who demanded a restoration of democracy and an end to the military regime that has been in power in their country for more than four decades. When the monks rose in revolt, taking to the streets in Rangoon and other cities, Western governments were vociferous in their support for the monks and argued for a continuation of the sanctions.

In India, the reaction was quite different. The country's petroleum minister had flown to Rangoon at the very height of the protests to sign a $150 million deal to explore for natural gas off the Burmese coast, and throughout the weeks of turmoil in Burma, the Indian government refused to criticize the junta. Instead, it put security forces in Manipur on a state of alert to make sure that Burmese protesters did not try to seek shelter on Indian territory, and when it appeared that anti-junta demonstrations might erupt in Moreh, it closed the checkpoint and declared a curfew in the town.

These steps were consistent with India's grand vision for the border territories it shares with Burma. This vision has a name, the "Look East" policy, and it indicates that after decades of obsession with the West, India is reorienting itself, turning toward China both as a trading partner and as a rival power. India's engagement with the Burmese junta is part of this policy, meant to check Chinese influence in the region and garner a share of the resources, especially the vast reserves of natural gas in the Shwe fields off Burma's western coast. After losing out to China in earlier contracts to extract Burma's petroleum and gas, India proposed a pipeline that would bring a portion of the Shwe gas into India through the northeast.

The pipeline was only one of many projects envisaged for the northeastern frontier, the most ambitious of which was the "Trans-Asian Highway," a network of roads connecting northeastern India with Southeast Asia and China, something last done during World War II. One of the segments of this highway would link Moreh to Mandalay in Burma, and then eventually to Mae Sot in Thailand, covering a distance of 870 miles. Supposedly, these projects not only would increase India's trade with its eastern neighbors; the improved transport network also would allow the extraction of natural resources in northeastern states like Manipur, bringing an end to the cycle of insurgency and poverty endemic to the isolated region.

All this sounded fairly plausible while I was in Delhi, but I couldn't help wondering whether it had any bearing on reality. I grew up in the northeast of India and had experienced for myself the discrepancy between life in the region and the things said about it in a faraway capital. When I had traveled in the past to the frontier between India and Burma, nothing I encountered there conformed to these visions of open borders and free trade. It had always seemed to me, from the time I lived in the northeast to when I moved away and began writing about it in my fiction, that there was something subterranean about the region, the sum total of its insurgencies, riots, and ethnic clashes never amounting to more than a few tremors in the larger world.

But it was possible that things had changed. India's friendliness toward the Burmese junta was a fairly recent development; before the right-wing BJP government of the 1990s, India had supported democracy movements throughout the developing world, including Burma, and allowed Burmese dissidents to cross the border and settle in Manipur. Since then, however, the BJP and the centrist Congress government that succeeded it have pursued their strategic interests in the region. No one spoke about the Burmese dissidents said to be floating around in Manipur, people who had escaped a harsh regime and fled to India, apparently with the idea that the Indian government would support them in their struggle for democracy. It was this invisibility that interested me, especially when measured against the "large-scale movement of peoples, ideas, and connectivity" being touted by India's prime minister, and so I headed for the borderland.

§

The flight from Delhi took a little over three hours, the densely populated Ganges plains giving way to a land of hills and ridges, still thick with forest cover, until the aircraft came down over the Imphal Valley with its small, rectangular agricultural plots and slender bodies of water edged with dark conifers. The Imphal airport building was new and clean, briefly raising the possibility that the official optimism had some substance to it, but then I stepped out into the open and found myself facing soldiers in black bandannas bristling around a ring of armored jeeps with gun turrets cut into their roofs. As for Imphal, Manipur's capital, it was just as I remembered it, with fetid drains, streets covered in rubble, and graceful women in striped *phanek* skirts who walked quickly past the soldiers posted at every corner.

The connection between the northeast and the rest of India has always been tenuous. Mountainous, lashed by the monsoons, peopled largely by groups described as "Tibeto-Burman," the region is attached to mainland India only by a thin strip of land squeezed between Nepal and Bangladesh known as the "chicken's neck." The geographical isolation is only one aspect of its difference. Six decades after a fledgling Indian government hastily took over these areas from the departing British, often against the wishes of the people living there, the northeastern states have a per capita income 30 percent lower than the rest of the country and an unemployment rate twice the national average. Four of the eight states in the region have significant insurgent groups fighting the Indian government, and sometimes one another, a situation to which the Delhi government has responded with the Armed Forces Special Powers Act, which gives security forces the right to arrest, interrogate, and kill without scrutiny from the notoriously corrupt local governments or from the courts.

Even by the standards of northeastern India, Manipur is an especially fractured state.* As with Kashmir, which it resembles in its violence and alienation from the rest of the country, its merger with India in 1949 is controversial, dependent on a document signed by the Manipuri king while he was under house arrest. The Lonely Planet guide to the region calls Manipur the most dangerous state in the northeast, hardly worth the trouble of applying for a permit to visit, as foreigners are required to do. In spite of the Armed Forces Special Powers Act, which has been in effect throughout Manipur since 1980, there are as many as twenty-three insurgent

---

* In May 2023, ethnic clashes erupted in the state between the dominant Meitei population of the valley and the Kukis in the hills. By July, at least 130 people, mostly Kukis, had been killed, and 60,000 displaced.

groups in the state, most of them operating from bases just across the border with Burma. Insurgents also control stretches within the sparsely populated hills, and during the two weeks of my stay, the smudgy print in the local newspapers gave accounts of gun battles and mine-clearing operations in Chandel district, where Moreh is located and where Indian forces were trying to dislodge an insurgent group from their "liberated" territory.

This general condition of turmoil, which people in Manipur seem to accept with resignation, lent a tinge of foreboding to my journey from Imphal to Moreh. The distance between the two towns is only sixty-eight miles, but it takes over four hours to make the journey by car, and even then one needs some luck. In the morning, just as I was heading out of my room, the hotel boy told me that no vehicles were being allowed into Moreh. I was told that a woman had been raped there the previous evening and that the Meira Paibi—a Manipuri women's organization originally formed in response to the brutal rapes and murders routinely committed by Indian soldiers—had shut the place down for the day. I headed out nevertheless, accompanied by a local photographer named Jinendra, who had pasted a very large PRESS sticker on the Maruti van I had hired. It was probably the sticker and the persuasiveness of Tomba, who was the driver of the van and also owned a small call shop* in Moreh, that got us past the first checkpoint, where dilapidated buses packed with people were being turned back by the police.

For a while, ours was the only vehicle on the highway, which wasn't much more than a narrow road bisecting paddy fields. Plumes of smoke rose from the fields where straw was being burned to create ash for the winter's crops, and in the distance were bluish-green mountains fringed with the unruly tufts of pine trees.

---

* A shop offering a landline payphone, necessary because cell phone signals are blocked by the government.

We passed small villages with open marketplaces and fortified police stations and army camps. Then we began climbing through the mountains, 10,000 feet at the highest point of Tengnoupal, and the road became an endless series of craters to be traversed behind long army convoys, the discomfort of the journey somehow negated by the thickly forested peaks and valleys, with patches of wild sunflowers exploding next to the rubble of the road.

§

On the highway from Imphal to Moreh, there had been a series of checkpoints where passengers and belongings were scrutinized, papers examined, and bribes paid. The most impressive of these was the checkpoint just before Moreh, sited along a bend in the road over which towered a paramilitary base on top of a hill. This was the place where, according to newspaper reports I had read in Delhi, three "Myanmarese nationals" had been stopped while they were headed toward Imphal. It was a border within a border, complete with a 600-foot stretch of no-man's land that people had to cross on foot, keeping their hands empty and leaving all their belongings behind in the vehicle for a separate inspection. Then our cell phones stopped working, apparently because the Indian government jammed signals inside Moreh. It wasn't entirely clear what purpose this served, but in a town where land lines were few and unreliable and everything was shut down by an evening curfew, it meant that one was completely cut off at night.

When I visited the Moreh police station, the officers there claimed to know nothing about the three "Myanmarese nationals," just as they could tell me nothing about the time when Moreh had been a center for Burmese activists. For that, I had to go and see a man I'll call Narayan. The local reporters who led me to him described Narayan as an influential local businessman who had organized money and material support for the dissidents, although he did not project such an image when I first saw him sitting on a plastic chair in the courtyard of a Hindu temple. A portly man in his fifties with wavy graying hair and a small mustache, Narayan had an air of calm reserve about him, and the only signs of emotion he displayed as he listened to my questions were the furrows of caution appearing on his brow. He seemed to be considering how much to tell me, and although I had been introduced to him by people he knew well and it was unlikely that anything I wrote about him would make its way to Moreh, he asked me not to use his real name because he didn't want to be identified by the Burmese junta.

Like most of the Tamils in Moreh, Narayan belonged to a diaspora descended from the traders and laborers who had gone to Burma from the southern Indian state of Tamil Nadu in the early twentieth century. He grew up in Mandalay and studied engineering, but after running a small business in motor parts, he decided to leave Burma in 1984, when it became increasingly difficult for him to continue his business. After trying for a while to live in Madras, now Chennai, the capital of Tamil Nadu, he settled in Moreh. "It used to be a nice place," he told me, perhaps detecting my disbelief that someone would so willingly leave a metropolis for a seedy border town. "But it became bad in the early nineties. Violent." This was the period when Manipuri insurgents belonging to different ethnic groups were attempting to take control of the town and its trade in narcotics, guns, gems, and teak. Some of these groups were supported by Indian intelligence agencies if they were thought to be a useful counterforce to a more troublesome outfit. As the Manipuri insurgents based in Burma turned Moreh into a battleground, they displaced the largely nonviolent Burmese dissidents who had sought shelter in the town, in Indian territory. The Indian government wasn't too perturbed by the exodus of Burmese dissidents; it had supported them in the past, but since forging a closer relationship with the junta, the government had begun considering them an irritant.

"There are no dissidents here anymore," Narayan said, sounding bitter. "No support for any Burmese working against the junta. There was a divisional commander who tried to defect a few months ago, but they handed him back to the Burmese army." The junta had benefited the most from the changes in Moreh, Narayan felt. They had won the Indian government over to their side, in part by promising to act against the insurgents operating from Burma, but they also used the Manipuri insurgents to do their bidding in exchange for providing them shelter.

I asked Narayan why he stayed on in Moreh, especially since he now owned a house in Chennai, one of India's booming cities. Narayan looked around and pointed at the temple. It consisted of a series of small shrines, each of them guarded by pairs of menacing, four-armed figures. It was unlike any temple I had ever seen, and Narayan explained that it had been modeled on a temple in Rangoon. It reflected the intermingling of Tamil and Burmese cultures that had taken place among the diaspora and that made this corner of Southeast Asia Narayan's own. This was what had kept him in Moreh, amid other Tamils from Burma, and he was closer to home here than he would ever be in Chennai.

But the nearness to Burma was an illusion. Narayan had started visiting Burma again when a recent power struggle within the junta deposed the minister in charge of internal security and destroyed many security files, making him feel that it was now "reasonably safe" to make the trip once a year. When he went to Burma, though, he traveled the long way around, going to Chennai first and then flying to Rangoon. I asked him if he had ever attempted to visit Burma from Moreh. "I would never attempt to go that way," he said. The Burmese authorities "know everybody here. They know me. Everybody knows everybody here," he said, and looked nervously at Jinendra, who had accompanied me to the temple.

§

The officially sanctioned border trade between Moreh and its counterpart, the Burmese town of Tamu, began in 1995. This was at the very start of the Look East policy, and the Indian and Burmese governments agreed to keep the checkpoint open during the day for the locals' convenience. Indeed, when I was there I saw people swirling through the border checkpoint, going past the Burmese guards to the Namphalong bazaar, the market on the other side, where stalls housed in a gray concrete building offered shapeless winter jackets, lighters with attached flashlights, and pirated DVDs in thin plastic sleeves. On the outskirts of Moreh, bullock carts filled with sacks of rice forded a small stream, right underneath a slum on the edge of a cliff where a boy was plucking a headless chicken, releasing clumps of feathers into the water down below.

But the gun battles, kidnappings, rapes, and bomb blasts that are regular incidents in Moreh and Tamu suggest that there is much more than an everyday exchange of goods going on in these places, as do the restrictions that increase in severity as one travels toward Burma. When I visited Tamu the next day, I had to leave my Indian passport at Tomba's call shop. It was the only government identification I possessed, but its foreign visas would draw attention to me as a person who had ventured beyond the northeast. Tomba took the passport and my cell phone, and made me empty my wallet of credit cards, debit cards, library cards, store receipts—all those talismans of globalization. Sometimes the Indian army came around to check his shop, so he put everything together with a rubber band and placed the collection in the refrigerator.

We were joined near the checkpoint by a local stringer I'll call Ibomcha. (Because the junta scans the foreign press for articles on Burma and this stringer often crosses the border, I haven't used his real name.) I was asked to stay in the background while the Manipuris gave their identity cards to the border guard, a man in an old khaki uniform and thick glasses who was laughing at whatever it was Ibomcha was saying. We walked away from the guard's post, making our way through the crowd milling around the checkpoint, still one permit short. The plan was made clear to me as soon as we were some distance away from the guard. Ibomcha would go back to Moreh from here, but I would travel on to Tamu with his permit, collecting his ID card on the way back. It was a deceptively simple trick, one that put my companions in high spirits, but the junta could afford to be lax about such small things. The barriers were in place long before one reached the Burmese border. Most of the people who crossed here were local, known to the junta, as Narayan had pointed out. The countryside was sparsely populated, with guard posts along the road where the permits had to be shown, and in that flat landscape a lone bicycle rider was visible from miles away.

When we stepped out from the van into the downtown area of Tamu, it looked quite unlike Moreh. It was clean and pretty, the straight avenue lined with small shops, low houses, and a bright red pagoda. A group of laborers smoked cheroots near a park, a few shopkeepers sat behind their counters, and a solitary Buddhist monk walked from store to store with his begging bowl.

There was another Tamu somewhere around here, one in which Manipuri insurgents hid out, where brothels were staffed by HIV-positive women who could no longer find work in Thailand, and where narcotics were gathered, packaged, and prepared for shipment into India. According to the US Drug Enforcement Administration, Burma is the second-largest producer of heroin in the world, and much of that business has shifted from the Thai border, after a crackdown by the Thai government, to the western border with India. The trade has brought to Tamu an ethnic group called the Wa, former headhunters and anti-junta guerrillas from Burma's northeastern frontier with China. Since signing a cease-fire with the junta in 1989, the Wa have been able to run narcotics and prostitution rings throughout Burma, and their interest in Manipur coincides with greater restrictions on the borders with China and Thailand. The heroin and amphetamine pills pumped into Manipur through Tamu and Moreh have devastated the state, which, with a population of only 2.4 million people, has the highest concentration of HIV cases in India, most of them injecting drug users.

The degree of control and surveillance in the town has ensured that even Manipuri journalists, used to threats and violence while working in their home state, do not attempt to report anything from Tamu. When Tomba said that we might be able to speak to a Burmese trader he knew, I wasn't particularly hopeful. We approached a house with a hardware shop on the ground floor and living quarters above, and an elderly man in a lungi came down to meet us. Tomba asked for the trader who lived there, but the elderly man shook his head. The trader was not at home; in fact, he had gone to Moreh, and if we hurried back, we might be able to meet him there. We went into some of the stores, but the shopkeepers, mostly women, avoided eye contact unless we showed interest in buying something. My companions began to trail behind me, and I felt alone and exposed. We had been the only non-Burmese people to get off the van ferrying passengers from the border checkpoint to Tamu, and no one else was wandering around these nearly empty streets. There wasn't even a tea shop in the downtown area where we could sit and look around, and it seemed only a matter of time before someone would appear to ask us for our papers, including my rather suspect permit with Ibomcha's name on it. The bluster that had been visible in Jinendra and Tomba at the checkpoint had evaporated, and when they began insisting that we should leave, I agreed.

On the drive back toward Moreh, we had a sudden glimpse of the Trans-Asian Highway, which we rode on for a few minutes before we turned off onto the dirt track to the Namphalong bazaar. The Trans-Asian Highway was a wide metaled road running from Tamu to Kalemyo, a distance of seventy-five miles. The signs on the road said that it had been built by the Indian army in an act of friendship between the two countries, and, according to the official junta newspaper, *The New Light of Myanmar*, the opening of the highway had been a ceremonious affair. More than 10,000 people had gathered in Tamu, accompanied by musical bands, to watch Lieutenant General Tin Oo (whose full designation was "Chairman of the Central Supervisory Committee for Ensuring Secure and Smooth Transport and Secretary-2 of the State Peace and Development Council"), Major General Saw Tun, and then Indian minister for external affairs Jaswant Singh cut the ribbon to open the road. I tried to imagine the Burmese cycles, makeshift motorcycle vans, and bullock carts—the only vehicles I had seen so far—making that journey to Kalemyo. The highway was utterly empty as we drove past.

When we returned to Moreh, I went to look at the highway from the other side, near a checkpoint closed to the public. There was a bridge spanning the stream that formed the border here, the Burmese half of the bridge painted yellow, the Indian portion in white. Another stretch of the highway was being built where I stood, and as I watched, a small, battered green truck made its way across the bridge toward us, bringing a load of stones to a group of Burmese women and children dressed in rags and makeshift turbans. The laborers waited until they had filled the baskets on their heads with rocks, and then they walked past me, going down to the stream to lay the foundations for this part of the Trans-Asian Highway stone by stone.

§

The last time such a highway had been built in the Indian northeast was in the 1940s, during World War II, when the battle for Asia turned in this obscure corner of the world. Manipur is where a Japanese army that had been victorious in China, Singapore, and Burma finally ran aground. Throughout the fighting, roads and bridges had to be laid in order for Allied soldiers and guns to be moved forward. It was a challenging task, one that briefly captured the imagination of the world, and the last time Manipur was mentioned in this magazine was in a 1944 article on the US General Joseph Stilwell's attempt to connect a different part of northeastern India, through Burma, with China. These were the roads that the Indian government was planning to rebuild for its thrust toward the east. When I arrived back in Imphal, I saw people wading through squelchy layers of refuse and plastic bags at the marketplace. The few restaurants had a shabby, secretive atmosphere, with most of the Indian customers looking like army men in mufti. As the sun set and wiry migrant laborers gathered around the small fires they had built on the streets, the buildings around them dark and silent, I felt as if I were in a postapocalyptic setting, but without any knowledge of how the end had come about.

§

I was planning to meet some Burmese dissidents who would tell me about their arrival in Manipur and how they had been affected by the Indian government's partnership with the junta. But when I called the phone numbers I had gathered in Delhi, the men who answered were suspicious and frightened. Eventually, I persuaded a man named Ko Thein to meet me, although he would see me only in my hotel room in Imphal. He showed up in the afternoon accompanied by another Burmese man, both of them looking awkward and uncertain as they stood in the corridor. My room, which cost six dollars a night, was a claustrophobic hole with fluorescent lights, its filthy windows opening onto a wall and a generator that spewed noise and diesel fumes into the room. The elevator in the hotel rarely worked, and at ten in the evening the entrance was closed off with metal shutters, locking residents and staff in and presumably keeping insurgents out. This was considered the best hotel in Imphal, popular because it had a restaurant and a conference room where small groups of people gathered during the day for seminars on business and governance. As the two Burmese men came in, hesitantly accepting my offer of tea and sitting gingerly on the two grimy armchairs, it seemed that what they saw in the room was luxury and power.

Ko Thein was a burly, shy man in a baseball cap; his friend Ko Todu was thin and light-complexioned, wearing glasses that had only one temple. Thein appeared to understand English but not speak it, whereas it seemed to be the opposite with Todu. We ended up in a complicated, three-way communication chain wherein I posed most of my questions to Thein, whose answers, translated back to me by Todu, I tried to write down as the generator pounded away in the background.

They had fled Burma in 1988, when the junta responded to a nationwide uprising on August 8 with a severe crackdown, killing at least 3,000 people and arresting thousands more. The Indian government had been supportive of the dissidents at the time. It looked favorably upon the Burmese democracy leader Aung San Suu Kyi, who had gone to college in Delhi and knew Rajiv Gandhi, then the Indian prime minister. The state-run All India Radio began a series of Burmese-language broadcasts that criticized the junta, while in Rangoon the Indian embassy gave medical aid and money to many of the activists, encouraging them to escape to India if they feared arrest. Thein and Todu made their way to Moreh, where the Indian government welcomed them with food and temporary shelter. After a few months, a camp was set up for the Burmese in the barracks of the Manipur Rifles, a paramilitary unit, at a place called Leikun, in Chandel district.

The dissidents who had fled to Moreh were hoping to launch an armed struggle from India. A militant organization called the All Burma Students' Democratic Front (ABSDF) had already been formed by exiles on the border between Burma and Thailand, with a fighting peacock as its symbol (which reappeared on the streets of Burma during the September 2007 demonstrations). The ABSDF members in Manipur thought they would start a guerrilla army, with training and equipment from India. But the Indian government made it clear that it didn't want another armed group operating in Manipur, and it ordered the Burmese dissidents to stick to nonviolent methods. I asked the two men if they had tried to go ahead with their armed movement in spite of the warnings, but they shook their heads. They couldn't have taken on both the junta and the Indian government, and they had known nothing about the complexity of the northeastern region they had fled to. "The Manipuri people have been good to us. They support our democracy movement," Thein said. "But the Manipuri insurgents are based in Burma and work for the junta. They would attack us here if we tried to form an armed group." Even though they were members of a nonviolent group, pressure from the insurgents had led Thein and Todu to leave Moreh. Two men who had last tried to operate from Moreh had been abducted from the town. "It happened late at night, on January 14, 2006," Thein said. "It was done by Burmese soldiers who came into Indian territory, but they were shown the way by Manipuri insurgents. On their own, the Burmese wouldn't have known where to find our men."

He glanced at Todu, who began feeling inside his torn puffy jacket and extracted a compact disc. I slipped it into my laptop and looked at the documents and pictures on the disc, including a plaintive letter to the deputy commissioner of Chandel district about the abduction in Moreh. The letter had obviously gone unanswered, but the disc was a surprise, suggesting forethought and organization, with information ordered carefully into letters, spreadsheets, and photographs, even though the lives they documented appeared very hard. The people in the pictures, including the two men who had been abducted, looked shabby, lost, and worn down by their long stay in Manipur. Three of the dissidents, all in their forties, had died in the past few years. "Heart trouble," Thein said.

According to Thein, there were a hundred dissidents or "political" Burmese left in Manipur, as distinct from the Burmese migrant workers who have been coming into Manipur since the nineties. The dissidents were divided between Imphal and Leikun, but in their years of exile they had married among themselves and had children. There were no schools near Leikun, and the ones in Imphal were unaffordable, so all the children of school age and their mothers lived in Churachandpur town, forty miles from Imphal. It seemed, in fact, that the lives of the dissidents were preoccupied less with protest than with survival. The guerrillas manqués had been forced to become entrepreneurs, collectively running a photocopying and call shop in Imphal and operating a van between Churachandpur and the neighboring state of Mizoram. Thein and Todu seemed embarrassed when they told me this, and Todu began laughing. "We are very bad businessmen," he said. "We took loans to buy the van, but now we can't pay them back."

They were anxious that I would think of them simply as refugees or failed entrepreneurs, and they told me that they operated a network across the border and organized camps in Manipur for people coming over secretly from Burma. In these camps, Thein said, they trained people in democracy, human rights, and "hygiene." But I think he realized even as he was talking to me that none of this sounded as dramatic as running camps for guerrilla warfare. "It's important we do this," he said. "We wanted to become guerrillas. That's why we came. But we couldn't, not without some help." He held out his large hands to me, as if demonstrating his willingness to carry a gun. "We get information about what's happening in Burma and pass it on to the world. The Thai border is full of Western media and NGOs, but they can't come here, and if we didn't stay here, no one would get information from this side. During the demonstrations in September, we got hold of photographs and stories that showed what was going on inside, and we helped people who tried to escape the junta."

It sounded as if the two of them were trying very hard to emphasize their role as dissidents, and they brought to mind a meeting I had attended that September of Delhi's Burmese dissidents and their Indian supporters. What was most evident at the meeting was the despair over the Indian government's cessation of support for the Burmese democracy movement. It was also clear that the dissidents had few ways of pressuring the Indian government. Instead, it was the three Indian representatives of Amnesty International who came up with a series of measures their office would take to publicize the Indian government's position, but they left before the meeting had come to an end, presumably to put these ideas into practice. It wasn't surprising that the Burmese dissidents didn't possess the same clinical efficiency as the NGO workers. The dissidents had been overtaken by history, by the change in India's attitude toward Burma, which in turn reflected how India's notion of foreign policy had become, in the past decade, mostly about securing its business and strategic interests. But a world that stressed markets over democracy paradoxically attached much more value to the category of political exile than to that of economic migrant, which explains why Thein and Todu had brought along their disc, hoping to show me that their lives included resistance as well as privation. There are nearly 50,000 Burmese in Manipur and Mizoram, most of them toiling in low-wage jobs involving seasonal agricultural labor, and they didn't want to disappear into this indefinable mass of the poor and the dispossessed. They had been middle-class in Burma, people with education who could have looked forward to government jobs and a certain degree of security. But they had given up on that future twenty years ago, and in return they insisted on their status as dissidents, as people still fighting for a cause.

§

A few days after Thein and Todu came to see me, I set off for the Leikun refugee camp in Chandel district. No one I knew in Manipur had been there. Isolated and forgotten, a remnant of the Indian government's earlier non-aligned phase of foreign policy, the camp seemed to stand in opposition to the transnational highway that would blast open this part of the world. Tomba drove, while Jinendra and I sat in the back. We turned off Highway 39 near the first Moreh checkpoint, heading into the mountains in Chandel district where the army was engaged in its operations against a

Manipuri insurgent group. The villages we passed were sparsely populated, with a few people clustered around a market or bus stop. Soon we had to slow down at a bend where a dozen trucks were parked, tarpaulin-covered civilian vehicles bookended by military escorts. There were troops in flak jackets, some of them shouting into walkie-talkies and others directing a vehicle up a steep track to the right. We were waved on, passing so close to the soldiers that I could read the names on their uniforms as we drove by.

The Manipur Rifles camp was a row of long buildings behind a brick wall and barbed wire. Jinendra spoke to the guard and went inside while Tomba and I waited by the road, exchanging small talk with the soldiers. We stood around for a while, far longer than it took to get directions, and I thought Jinendra was having trouble getting permission to proceed. Dusk was setting over the road, creating sharp silhouettes of the village women trudging up the mountain with cane baskets slung on their backs. Everything was quiet until two jeeps came back from a patrol, the camp gates swinging open as they raced inside. A few minutes passed, and then there was a sudden burst of activity inside the camp, with many uniformed figures waving and shouting at us. The gates swung open again, and we drove in, following a pair of tire treads cut into the grass. Our van groaned along, shrubs and grass scraping its belly, Tomba gripping his wheel tightly as we kept going along the mountain, the land falling away steeply to our right. We stopped where the tracks came to an end in the thick brush.

After the sound of the engines, the silence was startling. The last tinge of sunlight was nearly extinguished over the pine trees on the mountains. Below us was a valley, with terraced farmland giving way to jungle broken up by streams. On the other side, where the land rose again, was the Leikun camp, a scattering of huts with mud walls and tin roofs set in a clearing in the jungle. We walked down to the valley, crossing a gully bridged by a narrow, precariously placed log, wading through grass and pools of water before we began climbing up steps cut roughly into the earth. The furious barking of dogs and squawking of geese greeted us as we entered the camp. There was just enough light in the sky to see the two halls around which the smaller huts were arranged, the glow of wood fires showing through the halls' narrow doorways.

§

A thin man in jeans who had appeared at the sound of the dogs was asked by the Manipur Rifles sergeant to fetch the "village chief." I liked this designation for the camp leader; it suggested that the sergeant held on to an older, more humane idea of the refugee camp as a village and the Burmese exiles as just another tribe in this diverse land. Yet when the chief appeared, a slight, young man in rolled-up jeans holding a cell phone, the sergeant ordered him roughly into the hall that served as both a kitchen and a dining room. We crowded around the long dining table, wood smoke in our eyes. The sergeant grabbed the chief by his shoulders, shook him, and said, "There's a journalist who's come here from Delhi, understand? Sit down and answer all the questions."

Ney Myo was strikingly handsome, with long wavy hair and a delicate, almost feminine face. It couldn't have been easy for him to have so many strangers, three of them soldiers, barge into his camp at a time when everyone was preparing for bed. But he seemed spirited, responding directly to my questions and not hesitating to criticize the Indian government in front of the soldiers. The youngest of the dissidents I met, he had been fourteen years old when he fled Burma a year after taking part in the 1988 demonstrations. As Myo told me about his journey to India, patiently repeating the details and spelling out names, I realized that he had taken a route that coincided with the Trans-Asian Highway, escaping from Rangoon, through Mandalay, to Moreh.

Myo lived in Moreh for six months and then moved to Leikun. The camp wasn't what he or the other dissidents had expected: a place where they would be trained to fight the junta. Instead, the dissidents were prevented from going out without permission from the Manipur Rifles. They were treated like undesirable refugees, and this led to hunger strikes, protests, and a retort from an Indian officer that they were in a military camp where the rules of democracy did not apply. Some of the more troublesome dissidents were taken forcibly from the camp and abandoned near the border; some were arrested for venturing out of the camp and sent to prison in Imphal; some of them eventually left for Delhi, where recognition from the United Nations High Commissioner for Refugees might open up the prospect of political asylum in the West, mostly in Norway; and others went back to Burma. After a few years, the restrictions were unofficially eased, and those who still remained at Leikun began venturing out into the surrounding villages.

From the look of the mountains, the appearance of the local people, the violence between insurgents and government, and the isolation of Manipur from the world at large, they could have still been in Burma. They began weaving cloth, raising poultry, and gathering firewood to sell to the local people, living off the land like settlers on a frontier. But they never forgot that they were dependent on the goodwill of the local people and the patronage of the Indian government, which provided the camp inmates with eleven basic food items, each calculated to the kilo. Myo's responsibility as camp leader involved going to Chandel town once a week to collect these items, but he sometimes traveled to Imphal, where he met with other dissidents and picked up course materials for his correspondence degree in public administration. He was married and had two children, but he saw his family only when they came to Leikun during the school holidays.

After twenty years, Myo still considered himself a dissident waiting for the junta to collapse. "We have the option of getting Indian citizenship," he said, perhaps rather optimistically. "But we won't do that. It's been a good country for us, but we plan to return to a free Burma." Myo didn't agree with my suggestion that the dissidents were making things harder for their children, who were cut off from both India and Burma, possessing no rights in India other than that of residence and no memories of Burma. They couldn't even read or write Burmese, as Myo reluctantly admitted.

The soldiers were now growing impatient, and Jinendra and Tomba were worried about traveling back to Imphal in the dark. I wanted to see some more of the camp before we left, so Myo led us out of the kitchen toward the community hall. A little antechamber in the hall held a shrine with a small statue of the Buddha, who had a surprised look on his face. There was also a bulletin board on the wall, and one of the pictures showed five smiling Burmese dissidents dressed in camouflage uniforms, a vestige of their dream of an armed struggle.

Myo was talking about another uprising that would take place in 2008, one that would finally overthrow the junta. "What will you do if that happens and you can go back?" I asked him.

"The first thing I want to do is see my parents, if they are still alive," he said.

We had come out of the hall and were standing in the clearing, the mountains all around us. Although Myo spoke of going back soon, it seemed to me that Leikun was his journey's end. The camp wasn't the way station the dissidents claimed it to be, a temporary halting place and base for the eventual victorious return to Burma. It looked like a rough, makeshift home, a place where the '88 Generation would spend another twenty years as they had spent the first twenty, dwindling into nothingness.* "The next time you come," Myo whispered to me, "let me know first. There is a different way in, one that avoids the Manipur Rifles camp." He seemed so hopeful at the prospect of my return that I didn't tell him there wouldn't be a next time. Nobody other than the Manipur Rifles personnel visited the inmates, which was probably why the soldiers had been so excited to guide a stranger to the camp at the end of their working day. Nobody else was likely to show up in the future to meet the inmates of Leikun and listen to their stories. The lonely journey back from the camp made this clear enough, as we crossed the valley and came out of the Manipur Rifles base. It was dark all the way back to Imphal until we were pulled over at a police post, and all we could see then were the flashlights on our faces.

---

* Democracy would briefly be restored in 2015, when the National League for Democracy, led by Suu Kyi, won a decisive majority in the national elections and was allowed by the military to form the government. Foreign capital – often accompanied by foreign capitalists – began to flow in openly, even as Suu Kyi and the NLD defended the military against accusations of genocide against the Rohingya minority. The violence against the Rohingya, which continues, reached brutal proportions, displacing a million to neighboring countries, including Bangladesh and India. In February 2021, as the COVID-19 pandemic began to spread through the globe, the Burmese military carried out a coup, arresting Suu Kyi and NLD elected officials and returning itself to power.

PART II

Chapter 4
Manufacturing Foreigners

India's War of Disenfranchisement against Muslims

One November morning in 2015, a thirty-seven-year-old woman named Sahera Khatun received a notice summoning her to a foreigners' tribunal.* Sahera was living at the time in Sukharjar, a riverine village in the remote Indian state of Assam. She had moved there from Morabhaj, where she was born, after her marriage to a daily wage laborer named Amir. Sahera had given birth to five children in Sukharjar and seen nothing of the world beyond these two villages and the temperamental rivers that regularly inundate huts and farmland there. Yet the summons required her to prove that she was a citizen of India and not an illegal migrant from the neighboring country of Bangladesh. If she failed to make an appearance, the tribunal would declare her a foreigner and arrest her.

On the appointed day, Sahera and her husband made the two-hour journey in a crowded tempo to Foreigners' Tribunal No. 6, in the town of Barpeta. It was the first of many such appearances. Over the years, with the help of lawyers working pro bono, Sahera submitted a series of documents, including land records, copies of

---

*   First published in the *New York Times Magazine*, September 15, 2021.

electoral lists, and a marriage certificate. She was cross-examined by the official, as was the chief of the village she lived in.

In June 2018, the tribunal delivered its verdict. Sahera, on her lawyer's advice, stayed away, as she was likely to be detained if the verdict went against her. She was unable to state when she was born, at what age she married, or how old her parents and grandparents were when they first voted, the tribunal official noted. The documents she submitted were considered inadequate and untrustworthy, as was the testimony of the village chief. The tribunal ordered the police to take her into custody as an "internee" until she could be deported.

I met Sahera this year in the village where she is now hiding. It is a fertile area an hour's drive from Barpeta town, with huts built of corrugated tin looking down on fields lush with rice, corn, potatoes, and garlic. In the monsoons, the nearby Brahmaputra River—which originates in Tibet to the north and makes its way through Assam and into Bangladesh to the south—floods the fields. The tin shacks, blazing hot in the summer months, are easy to dismantle should the river rise high enough to inundate the embankments on which they are erected.

As I was led into a room with a dirt floor, neighbors began to crowd in, faces taut with wariness. A folder thick with papers lay on a plastic table. Sahera's lawyer had appealed the tribunal decision with the high court in Guwahati, the seat of government in Assam. But the high court upheld the tribunal verdict, and the case of *Sahera Khatun v. the Union of India* will now have to be heard at the Supreme Court in New Delhi. Sahera is already a fugitive. If the Supreme Court also rules against her, no one can say what might happen to her.

The neighbors waited outside while I spoke to Sahera and her husband. Amir did most of the talking, speaking softly in Bengali. Sahera, her face turned away from me, wept silently under the hood of her sari. Amir, whose own citizenship was not in dispute, told me that he and Sahera knew no other country than the one where they lived and where their parents lived before them. They had migrated to this village from nearby Sukharjar because, like the village where Sahera grew up, it had been eroded by the Brahmaputra. It was a phenomenon so common that there was a word for people displaced by the river: *nodibhongo*, or, literally, "broken by the river."

Neither Amir nor Sahera had received any schooling, and they did not know how to read or write. Amir worked delivering goods on a pushcart until he fractured his left leg. Now he sold vegetables in the nearby market, worrying about Sahera, who had lost her appetite and been unable to sleep ever since the tribunal notice arrived. I pointed at the documents on the table, to Sahera's thumb impressions prominent among the endless text and legal seals. "We don't even understand what's written in there," he said.

Sahera is one of around 2 million people in Assam who have been rendered stateless. Many are Bengali Muslims, a vast majority of them marginal farmers and daily wage laborers, who have nonetheless become the focus of a sustained campaign of disenfranchisement by Prime Minister Modi's Hindu nationalist government, led by the BJP. Portrayed as illegal migrants from neighboring Bangladesh, they have become mired in a Kafkaesque system of accusations, trials, and imprisonment, which in turn has spawned a nationwide citizenship act compared by commentators in India and the West to Nazi Germany's Reich Citizens Law.

The Hindu right has long identified border regions like Kashmir and Assam as places to raise the specter of a Muslim threat. But while Kashmir has often been used to conjure the danger of secession, Assam represents, in the rhetoric of Hindu extremists, a more insidious menace—that of a steady, cross-border influx of

Muslims guaranteed to make Hindus a persecuted minority in their own country. Assam is largely peripheral to historic Indian civilizations as well as to modern India—Guwahati lies more than 1,000 miles east of Delhi, with China and Myanmar far closer. Yet Assam has become central to the question of who is—and who is not—entitled to be a citizen in India.

In July 2018, Assam published a National Register of Citizens (NRC) that was intended to be a definitive record of citizenship. Any resident of Assam whose name did not appear on it would have to go before a foreigners' tribunal to plead their case: they would have to prove that they were born in Assam before 1971, when Bangladesh gained independence from Pakistan and refugees flooded into the state, or that they were the child of such a person. If the tribunal declared them foreigners, their only recourse was the courts. The "national" in the NRC is, however, misleading. It applies only to the state's multiethnic population of some 33 million, a third of whom are Muslim, although Modi threatened to create a similar citizens' register for all of India. When the initial version of the NRC was released, the names of nearly 4 million people were left off and their citizenship put in question. Amit Shah, then the BJP's president and Modi's able lieutenant, declared that these *ghuspetiyas*—a Hindi word for "infiltrators," widely understood to be a derogatory code word for Bengali-speaking Muslims—would be deported to Bangladesh.

As those omitted from the NRC wrestled with how to prove they belonged in Assam, a "final" version of the list was produced in August 2019, this time excluding 1.9 million people. But the BJP discovered that it had run into a snag. The process of creating the lists had been expensive, confusing, and traumatic—people killed themselves after discovering they were not on them—and prompted special rapporteurs at the United Nations to raise questions about their discriminatory nature. Of the nearly 2 million people potentially rendered stateless, many were Bengali Hindus as well as Bengali Muslims. This posed a problem for the BJP, which regarded Bengali Hindus, a significant group in the rest of India and a majority population in the Indian state of West Bengal, as essential to their majoritarian nation of 1 billion Hindus.

By December 2019, the BJP had passed a nationwide law to get around this problem—the Citizenship Amendment Act. The CAA would allow Hindu, Christian, Jain, Buddhist, Sikh, and Parsi migrants from Afghanistan, Pakistan, and Bangladesh to claim Indian citizenship and, in theory, allow Bengali Hindus excluded from the NRC to apply for citizenship too. Pointedly, the only major religious group in the region excluded by the CAA were Muslims.

This spring Assam held state elections, with the BJP campaigning fiercely to maintain its majority coalition in the state legislature. A win would mean even more Bengali Muslims swept into NRC-like dragnets. Already, the future for those caught in what has been described as the largest mass disenfranchisement project of the twenty-first century looks bleak. The foreigners' tribunal declaring Sahera an illegal migrant had ordered her to be kept as an "internee" until she could be "deported" or "pushed back" to "her specified territory," but Bangladesh refused to accept Assam's mass of newly rejected Bengalis as its citizens. They might not be wanted in Assam and in Modi's India, but there was no place they could go.

§

I first came to know of Sahera's plight at the law offices of Aman Wadud in Guwahati. It was February, and anxieties about the coronavirus pandemic had, for the moment, given way to a fever pitch of anticipation about the upcoming state elections. A pink-and-blue bungalow sitting in a back lane off a large, green pond, Wadud's office gives off the sleepy, relaxed air of old Guwahati, a welcome contrast with the bumper-to-bumper traffic and construction dust that choke the main thoroughfares. It is here, with something of the convivial atmosphere of a college dorm, that Wadud and his fellow lawyers work on representing the people rendered stateless.

In addition to the 1.9 million people left out of the NRC list, some 150,000 people had already been declared illegal migrants by the system of foreigners' tribunals. Established in 1964 to hear the cases of those accused of being undocumented migrants, the tribunals went into overdrive during the years the NRC lists were being prepared. There may be an overlap between those left off the NRC lists and those processed through the tribunals, but because the records are separate, it is impossible to say. And more than one agency is involved in accusing people of being foreigners. Since the late 1990s, the election commission has been examining old voter records in Assam and marking out individuals as "Doubtful" or "D" voters. The names of these D voters are passed onto the border police, which in turn sends them to the tribunals. The border police, which has officers in local police stations, is tasked with identifying illegal migrants and carries out its own random checks on people. Those it considers to be lacking sufficient proof of citizenship are given a summons to appear at the tribunals.

The burden of proof is always on the accused, and the tribunals, run by lawyers appointed and paid handsomely by the government, are notorious for their hostility to the supplicants. The only point of clarity is that in a state where the dominant language, culture, and much of the upper bureaucracy is Assamese, a majority of those excluded are Bengali speakers, with particular hostility reserved for those who, like Sahera, Amir, and Wadud himself, are Bengali Muslims.

Wadud, who is thirty-five, has an intense, scholarly air until he begins to talk about cricket. He also happens to be among the exceptions in a community that—settled in the nineteenth century in Assam's riverine lowlands as farmers by the British colonial apparatus—is largely impoverished and undereducated. His father was a professor of Arabic, and Wadud himself studied law in Bangalore and interned in Delhi with the renowned civil rights lawyer Prashant Bhushan. Yet he recalled, with something between distress and bemusement, being called a traitor when going to high school in Guwahati. "I would pray for an India win in cricket," he said. "I had sketched an Indian flag on my arm. But to some people, I was still a Bangladeshi, a foreigner."

Wadud returned to Assam from Delhi in October 2013, in the wake of a clash between Bengali Muslims and Bodos—one of dozens of tribes that make up Assam's multiethnic society. The violence, which took place over two months in the summer of 2012, left at least 78 people dead and more than 300,000 in relief camps, the largest such displacement in post-partition India. In May 2014, Bengali Muslims were attacked by suspected Bodo militants near Manas National Park. Women and children were shot as they fled toward a river; people were thrown into huts that had been set ablaze. Survivors said that among their masked attackers were park rangers whom they recognized from their daily interactions, but the BJP, rapidly rising in Assam as a political force, portrayed the events as a clash between encroaching Bangladeshis and indigenous Bodos.

"There is absolute impunity when Bengali Muslims are killed," Wadud said, recalling his work setting up legal-aid camps in the area around Manas. He accompanied witnesses to court in Guwahati, but no convictions have yet resulted from the ensuing trials. Soon after, he was inundated with requests to take on foreigners' tribunal cases. "Every ethnic and religious group in

Assam migrated here at some point in history," he said. "But it is only the Bengalis, who traveled upriver, who are seen as outsiders."

Those who are declared foreigners find the legal process incomprehensible, Wadud said. Many of the accused are women, who typically marry young and are unable to inherit property. Without education, possessions, or a life outside the home, they have almost nothing in the way of documents to prove their identity: no school certificates or voting records or property deeds. This was probably why Sahera found herself in the crosshairs of almost every investigating body; marked as a D voter and judged a foreigner by a tribunal, her name never appeared in the NRC.

Wadud began reading out statements from the tribunal's verdicts. I was drawn to Sahera's story by a piece of sophistry in her case; the verdict noted that it was not clear if the *gaonburah*—the village chief—who said he had known the defendant since childhood meant the defendant's childhood or his own childhood. Couldn't the tribunal have asked the *gaonburah* whose childhood he meant when he was being questioned? "Exactly," Wadud replied.

Behind him, through the open windows, I could see gaunt, bearded men working on a neighboring building. Snatches of music drifted in, the lilting Bengali folk tunes of the lower Brahmaputra region. I would see the scene repeat itself, with slight variations, through the coming weeks—wiry, dark-skinned men doing low-paid physical labor. These Bengali workers are sometimes beaten up by a vigilante group called Veer Lachit Sena, which considers them outsiders who take jobs rightfully belonging to the Assamese. Wadud turned to follow my gaze. "All the work is done by us," he said. "The construction, the cleaning, the daily wage labor. The city survives on crops grown by us. But they are manufacturing foreigners."

§

The identification and removal of foreigners, accompanied by a sealed border with Bangladesh, has been a long-standing demand on the part of the Assamese, but it took Modi's government to merge Assamese nationalism with Hindu nationalism and begin the chain of events that would result in a nationwide citizenship law. The identity and culture of high-caste Hindu Assamese centers largely on the northeastern part of the Brahmaputra River valley where the Ahom dynasty ruled until the 1800s, an area commonly referred to as Upper Assam. Bengalis from the lowlands of the south are seen as a menacing foreign presence, threatening to overwhelm the province demographically.

The dominant Assamese are a mix of Tai Ahom who migrated from Southeast Asia in the 1300s, tribes that preceded them, and upper-caste Hindus who migrated from the Gangetic plains as Ahom society became increasingly Hinduized. In the early nineteenth century, Britain absorbed Ahom-ruled Assam into its Indian territories and encouraged Bengali speakers, both Hindu and Muslim, to settle this new frontier zone as farmers, laborers, and minor officials. Assam was administered as a part of Bengal until 1873, with Bengali imposed as the official language by the British. Assamese speakers found themselves marginalized. "Much of the anxiety among the Assamese springs from that time," Sanjib Baruah, a professor of political studies at Bard College, told me. Baruah, who in his columns for the *Indian Express* has often criticized the NRC process and the suffering it has caused, pointed out that both Bengali Hindus and Muslims were vastly more educated than the Assamese-speaking population during this colonial period. "All the desirable jobs were being taken by them," he said, "in part because Bengal had been colonized earlier and Bengalis were therefore much more familiar with colonial norms."

The creation of India and Pakistan in 1947, with the eastern wing of Pakistan neighboring Assam, produced a stream of Bengali Hindu refugees into Assam—my father among them. Another wave of refugees, both Hindu and Muslim, entered Assam when East Pakistan descended into civil war in December 1970, followed by the creation of Bangladesh in December 1971. "The refugee presence was visible everywhere in Assam at the time," Baruah said, adding that this influx of refugees triggered a huge protest movement referred to as "the Assam agitation."

The agitation targeted Bengali "foreigners"—who were suspected of voting in large numbers and skewing electoral results—and swelled through the late '70s and early '80s. Its gruesome highlight was the massacre of at least 2,000 Muslim villagers in the paddy fields around a town called Nellie. The Congress government then in power in Delhi responded with concessions to the Assamese agitators. An agreement signed in the mid-1980s promised that all those who crossed the border into Assam after midnight on March 24, 1971—a date chosen to exclude the stream of refugees from the Bangladesh war of liberation that began on March 25—would be identified and deported.

Delhi did little to enforce this agreement over the decades. Instead, its neocolonial approach—the exploitation of natural resources, like tea and oil reserves, and the treatment of Assam as a frontier zone to be defended against China—was soon met with an armed Assamese secessionist movement that demanded an independent Assamese nation. The Indian government moved quickly to suppress it, invoking the Armed Forces Special Powers Act to suspend all civil liberties and engaging in frequent arrests, torture, and extrajudicial executions of secessionists through the '80s and '90s.

In the late 1990s, S. K. Sinha, a former army general, was appointed governor of Assam and charged with overseeing counterinsurgency operations. He sent a report to New Delhi claiming that the "unabated influx of illegal migrants from Bangladesh" was a primary cause of the armed insurrection. Making a distinction between "Hindu refugees" and "Muslim infiltrators," he warned of a future in which Muslim-majority districts, backed by "the rapid growth of international Islamic fundamentalism," would demand a merger with Bangladesh, cutting off Assam, with its "rich natural resources," from the rest of India.

The report was merely official confirmation of how the Hindu right was beginning to channel Assam's nativist anxiety about Bengali-speaking "foreigners" into its own religious agenda. Throughout those years, the Hindu right worked tirelessly to fuse Assam's linguistic nationalism with its own majoritarian vision of a Hindu nation, in which Muslims would always be foreigners. Indeed, the decline of the secessionist movement would coincide neatly with the Hindu right's rise.

In 2014, campaigning to form the next national government in India, Modi addressed a crowd just days after the massacre of Bengali Muslims near Manas National Park. Using dramatic pauses, he promised that once he came to power, Bangladeshis in India would have to pack their bags and leave for good. Two years later, Modi was the prime minister, and the BJP won state elections in Assam for the first time, campaigning against a backdrop of graffiti depicting "invading" ants and crows and a slogan that promised an Assam "free of foreigners, free of corruption, free of pollution."

The National Register of Citizens soon became the centerpiece of the BJP's ascendance in Assam. The Supreme Court judge who set the register in motion was Ranjan Gogoi, an Assamese later promoted by the BJP to chief justice. And the BJP chief minister of the state, Sarbananda Sonowal, was a former member of an Assamese nationalist party, who in 2005 successfully petitioned the Supreme Court to require those accused of being foreigners to prove that they weren't—not the state to prove that they were. The NRC would also shift the burden of proof onto the accused. In one of the strikingly perverse rules around a process already capricious and brutal, individuals were allowed to demand, through "objection letters," the exclusion of names that were included on the first NRC list. No proof had to be given, and those sending the letters—200,000 such letters were dispatched—were not required to appear before investigating agencies. Those denounced, however, had to prove their citizenship all over again. Even as the NRC process was unfolding, those declared illegal migrants by the foreigners' tribunals began to be called into police stations and incarcerated. They were held largely in separate sections within existing prisons, but construction had also begun on a stand-alone detention center meant to house 3,000 inmates. Plans were drawn up to build ten more such detention centers with similar capacity. At the same time, the government said it would triple the number of foreigners' tribunals to nearly 300 and announced plans to computerize records and use biometric information to track the so-called foreigners in real time and ensure they received no state benefits.

It was not until the passage of the Citizenship Amendment Act in December 2019 that the BJP's painstakingly constructed merger of Assamese and Hindu nationalism came under threat. In seeking to ensure that Bengali Hindus left out of the NRC could demand citizenship through the CAA, the new law inspired fear among the Assamese that Bengali Hindus residing in Bangladesh would see it as an invitation to enter Assam in large numbers. Violent protests broke out in Assam against the CAA, with five demonstrators shot dead on the streets of Guwahati. Flights and long-distance trains were canceled, cellular and internet communications were suspended, and a curfew was imposed on the city while security forces set up roadblocks to frustrate the thousands of massed Assamese protesters.

Modi was reelected in May 2019 as prime minister with a sweeping majority; the protests against the CAA constituted the first major challenge to his authority. While Assamese demonstrators raged in the streets against the CAA and demanded an even more stringent NRC, crowds elsewhere in India gathered to protest both the CAA and the threat to expand the NRC to the rest of India. The BJP backpedaled, denying that the list produced in Assam was final or that the NRC would be expanded, but Modi himself remained silent. Eventually, as concern mounted that the NRC was merely a trial run for disenfranchising more than 200 million Muslims (the US Commission on International Religious Freedom, a bipartisan governmental advisory body, was calling for sanctions), Modi made a public appearance. Waving his hands and modulating his speech in the manner of a Bollywood star, Modi described talk of detention centers for Muslims as an outright lie and asserted that there was not a single one in all of India.

§

By the time I visited Lower Assam in February, the annual floods had come and gone. Villagers had been displaced along the Brahmaputra as usual, settling in temporary camps along the riverbank until they could return home and rebuild their shacks. Now there was the urgency of getting things done before the rains returned, and people trudged along the edge of the highway, picking their way through the sandbanks exposed by the receding water.

In Barpeta town, villagers who had been summoned to foreigners' tribunals, which were located in a shopping center filled with cell phone and electronics stores, waited in narrow hallways to be called inside. Others, mostly middle-aged women exhausted by a lifetime of physical labor and bewildered by the documents with official seals and stamps that they carried around in crinkled plastic bags, made their way to a small office where a group of activists known as the Miya poets would help them with their legal appeals.

Abdul Kalam Azad, one of the poets, told me that when the NRC process first began in 2010, a vast, impoverished majority were fearful of what might unfold. Huge public protests against the NRC had taken place in Barpeta, with four demonstrators shot dead by the police. Azad and his friends and other educated Bengali Muslims, however, saw the NRC as an opportunity, believing that, once complete, it would dispel any doubts over citizenship, giving Bengali Muslims definitive, state-sanctioned proof of belonging in Assam.

Many of the Miya poets were among the first generation to be formally educated—Azad himself is a former construction laborer who completed his undergraduate degree through a correspondence course and is now pursuing a doctorate—and they had faith in the power of papers, books, and ideas. They tried to help those far more fearful of bureaucracy and the state, traveling to the *chors*—the shifting river islands along the Brahmaputra—to assist the poor, unschooled inhabitants with the arduous paperwork.

As the process unfolded and the cruelties of the system became more evident, Azad and his friends grew more doubtful. Their unease fed their self-assertion as "Miya" poets—their name, an honorific for Muslim males, is commonly used as a slur in Assam—and their verses, inspired by the radical poetry of Gil Scott-Heron and Mahmoud Darwish, were often written in a dialect spoken by Bengali Muslims. Although Assamese readers initially responded favorably, supportive figures were soon drowned out by hostile voices. After a Delhi-based human rights organization made a five-minute video of Miya poets reading their work in July 2019, four separate criminal complaints were filed against ten of them. They were charged with posing a threat to national security, obstructing the NRC process, and defaming the Assamese people as "xenophobic in the eyes of the whole world." A television host summed up the prevailing sentiment: "If anyone from outside Assam sees this video, they will think a second Rohingya ethnic cleansing has started."

The charged atmosphere sent the poets into hiding—one was inundated with rape threats; another was warned that he would be killed—but by the time I visited them in Barpeta, their anxiety had given way to something like weariness. Between the first NRC list, which excluded 4 million, and the final one, which excluded half that number, Azad realized that he and his colleagues had made a mistake in not challenging the NRC from the very beginning. "None of us had the courage to oppose it," Azad said. "At one point, I began to feel guilty about telling villagers to fill out the forms. We showed them a dream when it was a trap."

A similar sentiment was expressed to me by Sulaiman Qasimi in Nellie, the place where, thirty years ago, 2,000 Muslims were massacred during the height of the agitation against so-called foreigners. Qasimi, who lost twelve members of his family that morning, had been listening while I spoke to a couple in their eighties who were incarcerated for almost five years after being declared foreigners. "Many Bengali Muslims aren't highly educated," Qasimi said. "They aren't big businessmen or landlords, and that is why they are sent to detention centers. These cases exhaust all the resources of our people, which means they have nothing left to feed and educate their children, which in turn means their children will never have the education to break out of this cycle."

That cycle was visible everywhere in Assam, but perhaps nowhere more starkly than on the river island I visited with Azad.

Birds skimmed off the river as we went out in a long wooden boat with a makeshift engine, clumps of dirt drifting in the water as reminders of the provisional nature of the *chors*. We passed a rowboat carrying a family, a boy at each end pulling on an oar, two girls and the parents huddled in the middle with bags of rudimentary supplies.

On Kapastoli *chor*, there was no clinic or electricity. The school was a drab concrete structure in which a villager called Faizal Ali hanged himself when he didn't find his name on the NRC. We met his two daughters, girls of eight and ten wearing clothes that were little better than rags. Their mother worked in Guwahati as a daily wage laborer. Their maternal grandfather, who had been declared a foreigner by a tribunal, had fled the island and was working as a rickshaw driver in Goalpara, where the first stand-alone detention center was being constructed. The girls had been taken in by extended family and made a living repairing fishing nets. They told Azad that they felt afraid to go near the school, knowing that their father died there.

As we walked on, a family invited us in for tea and told us that the original Kapastoli *chor* had been submerged years ago. The villagers gave this *chor* the same name when they moved here, a gesture strikingly human in its desire to maintain a sense of belonging but utterly futile in the face of the bureaucracy unleashed against them. Apart from the school and a concrete platform built as part of a government program, the state seemed utterly absent, and yet it was present everywhere as the all-encompassing regime of D voters, foreigners' tribunals, and the NRC.

§

More than $200 million has been spent on the NRC, but there is still no resolution to the question of who belongs in Assam. In

May 2019, the Supreme Court ordered the release of detainees who had completed three years in prison, as long as they paid a substantial collateral of nearly $3,000, had their biometrics recorded, and reported periodically to their local police station. During the first wave of the pandemic in April 2020, it ordered the release of more detainees.

Fewer than a thousand people now remain in detention in Assam. It is nevertheless unclear what will happen to those who have not yet been incarcerated—a majority of those declared stateless. Hiren Gohain, who is perhaps Assam's best-known progressive intellectual and a staunch critic of the Hindu right as well as of India's counterinsurgency practices, sees the NRC completed in August 2019 as the best solution to an inherently complex situation. He said he understood the frustrations of the Miya poets over how chauvinist sections of the Assamese were targeting Bengali Muslims. Nevertheless, he said, if there was to be any hope of reconciliation—a way to balance the competing claims of the various groups in Assam, including land-poor tribes and impoverished Assamese—Bengali Muslims had to have patience. "Ultimately, only 1.9 million were left out," he said when I met with him in Guwahati. Of those, Gohain went on, 1 million would escape punitive measures because they claimed ancestry from Indian states like West Bengal and Bihar, which had not responded to requests for documentation from Assam. "That leaves only nine hundred thousand," he said. "This does not mean a terrible injustice."

Gohain believes that those unable to prove citizenship should be allowed to go about daily life until they can be resettled but that they should not be allowed to vote. "There are resident aliens in every other part of the world," he said. "People who enjoy certain rights, but not the political right to vote." Other proposals that have been aired include denying declared foreigners access to government services, issuing them guest-worker permits, or redistributing the population to Bengali-majority states in India, like West Bengal and Tripura. Although put forward as humane alternatives to indefinite—not to say impractical—incarceration, these "solutions" are oblivious as ever as to those whose lives have been shattered.

The BJP leaders I saw campaigning one bright February morning in Bordowa, a picturesque village in Upper Assam, certainly seemed intent on increasing the number of the stateless. Bordowa is the hometown of Sankardev, an Ahom-era religious figure who gave Assam its distinct version of Hinduism, and it is part of a multimillion-dollar project by the BJP government to develop "religious and cultural tourism." As an Indian Air Force helicopter carrying Amit Shah, now the home affairs minister, touched down, unmasked crowds made their way on foot across emerald-green paddy fields toward the central stage. Much of Assam's multiethnic population seemed represented in the carnival atmosphere; the only people left out were the Bengali Muslim villagers I passed earlier, walking in the opposite direction and avoiding eye contact with the crowd.

Sonowal, Assam's chief minister at the time, opened the proceedings. But it was a minister in his cabinet, Himanta Biswa Sarma, speaking next, who, in a move meant to signal the BJP's confidence in its hard-line Hindu nationalist position in Assam, would be made chief minister after the BJP's victory there in May. At the rally, Sonowal's soft voice soon gave way to Sarma's testosterone-fueled speech, in which he worked in a denunciation of outsiders at every opportunity, pumping up the crowd by telling them that those attempting to occupy "sacred Indian soil" like that of Bordowa would never be forgiven by the people of Assam.

Finally, it was Shah's turn. Speaking in Hindi, he reminded the audience that his home state of Gujarat, on the other side of the subcontinent and over 1,200 miles from Assam, was connected by Hinduism to the "sacred land" of Sankardev. When the crowd's attention seemed to wander, Shah worked in his dog whistles. "The work of freeing Assam of *ghuspetiyas* was begun by the BJP government under Narendra Modi," he reminded the audience. A solitary Bengali Muslim man near me shifted uneasily in his seat.

The coming months featured plenty such reminders: billboards depicting barbed-wire border fencing as a BJP achievement, Sarma declaring that he did not need the Miya vote. The election manifesto released by the BJP made promises to every ethnic group in Assam except Bengali Muslims. Absent by name, they were the obvious targets of the section titled "Strengthening Civilization in Assam." This would be achieved by tackling the threat of "Love Jihad" and "Land Jihad," the manifesto stated, using the Hindu right's catchphrases for the supposed menace posed by Muslim men marrying Hindu women and by Muslims occupying land—acts intended, according to the Hindu right, to engineer a demographic shift. Along with this came the promise to "ensure the correction and reconciliation" of the NRC and a reinforcement of the system of border police and foreigners' tribunals.

With the BJP's victory in Assam this spring, the symbiosis of Assamese nationalism and Hindu nationalism seemed complete. Sarma, after becoming chief minister, promised a "reverification" of the list, particularly in areas bordering Bangladesh; names on the list would be subject to scrutiny yet again. The Assamese official in charge of the NRC, Hitesh Dev Sarma, petitioned the Supreme Court for permission to fully review the list, claiming it contained "glaring anomalies of a serious nature." (He declined to comment further for this article.)

"What corrections do they want to make?" Wadud said with anguish when I spoke with him after the elections. "This is cruel."

He was waiting for Sahera's case to come to the Supreme Court*, he said, but he felt that the struggle was becoming more uneven. He saw only more suffering ahead.

Work on the flagship detention center in the district of Goalpara, which has been under construction for more than two years, was proceeding steadily when I visited in February. Yellow watchtowers and staff quarters mark a vast perimeter of red walls, while sloping tin roofs demarcate the area meant for a medical center and a school for children who will be forced to accompany their internee parents. The women's section is as yet little more than a cordoned-off area, but the men's quarters are in an advanced stage of construction, three floors of dormitories rising into the blue winter sky. The only structures of comparable size in the area are the military bases squatting on the banks of the Brahmaputra, a reminder of India's brutal counterinsurgency operations in Assam.

Recently, the Assam government announced that detention centers would be renamed "transit camps," because that was more "humane." "You can't make it 'humane' just by changing nomenclature," Wadud told me. "The only way to humanize things is to stop detaining Indian citizens."

---

* As of July 25, 2023, Sahera's case was still being heard at the Supreme Court, with orders from the court that "no coercive steps" be taken against her in the meantime.

Chapter 5
Ram's Kingdom

The Ayodhya Temple
and the Ruins of History

Ayodhya, under the dirty gray monsoon sky, was a surprise and a disappointment.* All the way to this town in the northern state of Uttar Pradesh, the most populous, largest, poorest, and possibly most violent state in one of the most violent countries in the world, the promise of change had been insistent. It lay behind me, in the sheet metal cordoning off the heart of New Delhi and demarcating the $2 billion Central Vista project that will erect a new parliament complex and a new residence for India's prime minister, Narendra Modi. It glittered on the edges of the pristine, mostly empty airport at Lucknow, where I had flown in from Delhi, and along the freshly tarred highway that took me, in a four-hour drive, from Lucknow to the town of Faizabad. Most of all, it lay ahead, in Ayodhya, Faizabad's twin town, where Modi and his cohort of Hindu-right political groups are building a grand temple to the Hindu god Ram on the site of a destroyed mosque.

The new parliament will be complete in October 2022; the temple, in December 2023. In May 2024, Modi and his BJP

---

* First published in *Tablet*, April 7, 2022.

expect to win national elections for a third consecutive term. In 2025, the Rashtriya Swayamsevak Sangh (RSS), the 5-million-strong paramilitary organization that is the fountainhead of the Hindu right, will mark a century of existence. For a significant section of Indian society, all this, taken together, marks a beautiful convergence. It means that India is close to achieving its true self, a futuristic nation that has fulfilled, in spite of assaults by Muslims, communists, and the West, its grand promise as an ancient, supremely advanced, Hindu civilization.

The centerpiece of this millenarian fantasy is the 57,000-square-feet, three-story sandstone temple being constructed in Ayodhya. If the parliament complex is necessary to maintain the facade of India's democracy, the temple is of far greater resonance. It consecrates, supposedly, the birthplace of Ram, the blue-skinned, man-king-god who is the troubled protagonist of the epic poem *Ramayana*, composed between 200 BCE and 200 CE. Given that the temple is being built on the ruins of a sixteenth-century mosque—the Babri Masjid—constructed by the Mughal dynasty just coming to power then in the Indian subcontinent, the temple is intended as a mark of Hindu supremacy in India and perhaps of the beginning of the end of the Muslim presence here. As a local RSS official called Dr. Anil told me one morning, humanity itself originates in Ayodhya. Here is where the first man, Manu, was born after the great flood, along with the first woman, Satrupa, he said. This is where Ram was born, the ideal king of a utopian kingdom—Ramrajya—that will soon be revived on the Indian subcontinent.

And yet when I visited in August, Ayodhya-Faizabad was nothing more than a warren of muddy, waterlogged lanes and squalid buildings, the Ram temple just another hoax of the sort India has served up in plenty over recent decades. A model of the temple sat under a glass box in the reception of the hotel I was staying in. An ocher-colored complex of cupolas and spires, it appeared generic and unimaginative, completely adrift from the glorious temple architecture historically found in India. It is being designed by a Gujarat-based family close to Modi that specializes in contemporary Hindu temples, among them one in New Jersey raided last November by the FBI for using forced labor.

The hotel itself wallowed in sullen suspicion of its guests. The Canada-resident Indians who owned it had turned the white, once-elegant mansion—belonging to a former socialist legislator who had been defeated in 1948 by a Hindu-right smear campaign about his atheism—into a shabby sequence of rooms, the large windows in the corridor firmly shut against the red-bottomed monkeys marauding along the rooftops. The Wi-Fi worked, but only near the reception. There was no bar. Meals, strictly vegetarian, were served only in the rooms, and the bathroom floor was uneven, collecting runoff water from the shower and clumps of the plentiful mud I tracked back from outside.

The streets outside weren't much better. Apart from SUVs muscling their way through the chaotic traffic and the occasional smartphone in the hands of a passerby, nothing seemed to have changed over the past half century. The Muslim driver, a boy in his late teens whose only glimpse of a world beyond came from a brief stint driving trucks between Lucknow and Delhi, voiced his despair quietly as he guided the car through the streets. He wanted to get out, he said, but he didn't know how.

He drove me around and showed me the sights available for those who couldn't leave. There, he pointed out, was the *afim kothi*—the opium house—a haunted ruin of a mansion with crumbling boundary walls that marked the arrival of British colonialism in the late eighteenth century. The opium the peasants had been forced to cultivate had been exported to China, the descendants of the impoverished peasants shipped as indentured labor to Fiji and the Caribbean. Across from the opium house was the postcolonial Indian state's contribution to the memory of this violence, a vast, open dumping ground littered with garbage.

We moved on. There was the Gulab Bari—the "Pink House," characterized today by blackened onion domes and minarets, with echoing corridors where young Muslim men and women took selfies and a lone fakir silently contemplated the ineffable. A mausoleum for the eighteenth-century Shia Muslim monarch Shuja-ud-Daulah, it was built at a time when Faizabad had briefly been capital of Awadh, a tributary state to the Mughals. And there, finally, was the muddy brown Ghaghara River, which is called the Sarayu when it touches Ayodhya on its journey downstream. Ram had drowned himself in the Ghaghara around here, I was told; the temple to our left marked that event.

Rain came down hard on the new, slippery concrete paving the riverbank. People—priests, attendants, their families—napped inside the temple complex. Young men loitered outside, trying to find some pleasure in their surroundings, while ragged children scurried around selling peanuts and flowers. Most of all, the promenade seemed to belong to the cows, protected by a Hindu-right law that promises punitive measures against anyone "endangering their lives," a piece of legislation that has resulted in roving lynch mobs targeting those suspected of bovine endangerment. Bony, whitish, and dirty, the cows were scattered everywhere, depositing their shit wherever they wanted. I stepped on a pile of cow shit and went down. The driver helped me up and we stared at each other in silent, mutual, despair. There was nothing to say.

In 1984, with only two members in India's nearly 600-strong national parliament, the Hindu right seemed to have reached a terminal point in its turbulent history. Hindu political organizations had proliferated in the early twentieth century under

British rule, the most significant of them being the RSS. Funded and led by upper-caste men, the RSS combined ideas of Hindu revival spread by people like the late nineteenth-century monk Vivekananda with the racial theories increasingly popular in the West in the 1920s. M. S. Golwalkar, who became chief of the RSS in 1940 (and who is named by Modi as a major inspiration in his book *Jyotipunj*, or "Beams of Light"), wrote approvingly of Germany's "purging the country of the Semitic Races—the Jews," and urged Hindus to manifest a similar "Race Spirit" in regard to Muslims.

The end of colonialism in 1947 and the traumatic partition of the subcontinent into India and Pakistan allowed the Hindu right to carry out violent purges in areas where Hindus were a majority. At least a million people were killed, millions more displaced, hundreds of thousands of women and girls sexually assaulted, with Hindus, Muslims, and Sikhs all caught up in the spiral of suffering and hate. But soon after these traumas, the RSS appeared to run aground. On January 30, 1948, a Hindu extremist shot Gandhi dead for being too conciliatory toward Muslims and Pakistan. Although the RSS conveniently claimed that the assassin was no longer an active member of the organization, it was banned for a brief period and disappeared from mainstream public life.

As it turned out, being underground agreed with the RSS's cultlike tendencies. Even after the ban had been revoked, electoral maneuvering was left to its political front, the Jan Sangh—which morphed into the BJP in 1980—while the RSS focused on its ideal of building a patriarchal Hindu nation. It recruited boys between the ages of six and eighteen, using doctrinaire lectures, a distinctive khaki uniform, and a routine of paramilitary drills to mold their "Race Spirit." Individuals can be members of both the RSS and the BJP, and the latter's top leadership, including Modi, inevitably worked in the trenches with the RSS before making the move into parliamentary politics.

It was a combination of decades-long deep organizing with a massive public campaign that finally overcame the Hindu right's consistent electoral failures and handed it the keys to India. In December 1949, just as the Hindu right was emerging from the backlash that had followed Gandhi's assassination, a Ram idol appeared mysteriously inside the Babri Masjid. The Hindu right's version of this story was that Ram had manifested himself to seize back his birthplace; the more prosaic truth is that a Hindu monk from one of the most powerful monasteries in the area snuck the idol in, aided surreptitiously by sympathetic Hindu government officials. As tensions rose, heavy iron padlocks were placed at the mosque gates. A complex legal dispute followed, with Muslims as well as three rival Hindu monastic orders claiming the right to worship in the structure while idol and mosque slumbered more or less undisturbed through the coming decades.

In 1984, the Vishwa Hindu Parishad—the World Hindu Council—demanded that the mosque be torn down, claiming that Muslims had destroyed an ancient temple that commemorated the spot as the birthplace of Ram and built the mosque on top of it as an act of deliberate humiliation. There is no historical evidence that Ram existed; that present-day Ayodhya coincides at all with the celestial Ayodhya spoken of in the *Ramayana*; or that any other temple previously occupied the spot where the Babri Masjid was built. But the VHP—one of numerous Hindu-right groups affiliated with the RSS—was undeterred by these factual hurdles and demanded that a temple to Ram be built at the site. By 1989, its temple campaign was in full swing, with donations and *shilas*—bricks—being solicited from all over India and the wealthy Indian diaspora in Britain and the United States. Bricks to build the temple, some of them made of gold, wound their way across the country toward Ayodhya in long, ceremonial processions that were inevitably accompanied by violence. When the national elections took place that year, the BJP's share of parliamentary seats rose from two to eighty-five.

By the next fall, the temple-building campaign had moved up another notch. On September 26, 1990, L. K. Advani, the avuncular-looking president of the BJP, began a symbolic *rath yatra*—a chariot procession—across the country in a Toyota pickup outfitted as an ancient Hindu chariot. His starting point was Somnath, a town in Gujarat some 6,000 miles southwest of Ayodhya where a Hindu temple had been sacked in the eleventh century by a Muslim ruler from Ghazni, in present-day Afghanistan. The man in charge of organizing the procession was Narendra Modi, captured in photos as a brooding presence on the Toyota chariot. Like the procession of bricks, Advani's chariot and the *kar sevaks*, or volunteers, who planned to build the temple with their bare hands provoked sectarian rioting in the cities, towns, and villages they passed through. Advani was arrested before he reached Ayodhya, but *kar sevaks* already in town stormed the Babri Masjid on October 30. The ensuing police response led to the deaths of sixteen men, according to the official account, while the Hindu right claimed that more than fifty had been killed. Riots broke out all over India while the BJP withdrew support for the coalition government then in power in Delhi. When a fresh round of national elections was completed in the summer of 1991, the BJP increased its tally of parliamentary seats from 85 to 120.

The increasing electoral success of the BJP against the backdrop of escalating violence meant there would be one final move in this phase of its temple campaign. On December 6, 1992, while Advani and leaders of the BJP watched from a nearby rooftop, members of the Hindu right rushed the barricades around the mosque just as they had done two years earlier. Their numbers, this time, were far greater; the police were now partly intimidated and partly sympathetic to their cause.

Grainy footage from the time is available from the Indian television program *Eyewitness* and its reporter, Seema Chishti. It is just past noon, and thousands of men, some saffron-clad, clamber over the fence, banging away at the three domes of the mosque with whatever they have at hand: rocks, picks, hammers. In contrast to an early morning demonstration by RSS volunteers—purposeful, military—this is a crowd in a state of frenzy. Nevertheless, there is enough forethought to carry out the Ram idol and its canopy before attacking the mosque. It takes two hours for the first dome to collapse, another ninety minutes for the second dome to be brought down. In six hours, the entire mosque has been leveled to the ground.

Dr. Anil remembered the demolition and the events leading up to it as a time of great clarity. His father had been a "leader" in the Samajwadi Party (SP), which had opposed the temple project and was in power in Uttar Pradesh when the first group of *kar sevaks* arrived in Ayodhya in 1990. Dominated by the Yadav caste, a largely agricultural group, the SP's electoral success was built on an alliance between Yadavs and Muslims that challenged the upper castes consolidated around the Hindu right. Dr. Anil's father, who was upper-caste, was moved sufficiently by the fervor of *kar sevaks* passing through their village to nearby Ayodhya to switch political allegiance. "When he crossed the river, it was as a *kar sevak* to take part in the struggle against the mosque," Dr. Anil said.

Dr. Anil appeared to think of this transformation in his father as only natural, the coming to life of a higher principle. "When Ram was here, there was no Islam, no Christianity," he said. He would expand on that idea later, but that morning he was in a hurry to get the essential points of his life across. He himself had been loyal to the Hindu right from the beginning, starting as a member of the student wing of the BJP and eventually joining the RSS. Now he was the *prant prabhari*—the area chief—of the Rashtriya Muslim Manch, the Muslim wing of the RSS.

He seemed particularly proud of two achievements in this capacity. He had organized a ceremonial meal where Muslims had been served milk and fruit instead of biryani, the Persian-influenced dish of rice and meat more common on festive occasions. "Meat, fish, the eating of these things is a sin," he said. In the switching out of meat for fruit and milk, he clearly felt that he had in some sense briefly liberated the Muslims from their sinful existence and converted them into upper-caste, vegetarian Hindus. He had also convinced local Muslims to donate money for the construction of the Ram temple. "The soil is India," he explained. Ram was the ideal Indian, they were Muslims living in India: Where was the contradiction?

I hadn't known that the RSS had a Muslim wing, and I didn't know quite what to make of Dr. Anil. Slight, balding, with a gentle paunch and lively eyes, he didn't project the violence I associated with the RSS. He was a Kshatriya—the warrior caste—but it was hard to take him seriously as a combatant. He laughed a lot, although never at himself, and a boyish self-satisfaction radiated from him, remarkable for a man in his early forties. He had arrived at around eight in the morning in my hotel room carrying a motorcycle helmet, the very persona of a busy professional who started his days early and worked long hours. Dismissing my offer of tea because he was required, as an RSS man, to avoid all intoxicating substances, he filled the ugly, airless room with his soundbites: "The RSS is purely interested in the development of the nation, not individuals"; "The RSS is not a political party. It does not depend on the BJP"; "There is no casteism in the RSS." To this, he occasionally added the specifics of his personal story.

The "doctor" referred to his PhD in library and information sciences. He now worked as "guest faculty" at Dr. Ram Manohar Lohia University (a university named after an anti-colonial, socialist politician). He also owned a computer and photocopying business near the university.

It was possible to read these details as characteristics of an entrepreneurial multitasker dabbling in politics, education, and business, someone exemplifying the energies that have been unleashed in Modi's India. But then, there was the fact that, like almost everyone else I sought to interview, Dr. Anil came to the hotel room because there was nowhere else to meet in Faizabad-Ayodhya, no cafés or bars or restaurants offering the possibility of a social life. His guest faculty position had been terminated fifteen days earlier because he had come to the end of a four-year contract; he had massive debts and his business wasn't going well; he had pulled his daughter—the youngest of three children, the other two being boys—out of school because he didn't have money for the fees and didn't believe she was learning anything anyway.

The harsh truth about Ayodhya seemed to be that very little had changed there for the better even if the temple-building campaign had made its effects felt all over India by fueling the rise of the Hindu right throughout the country. Modi, in particular, seized on it, taking its combination of violence and spectacle further by giving it the distinctive stamp of his paranoid personality. In February 2002, on the tenth anniversary of the demolition of the Babri Masjid, fifty-nine *kar sevaks* returning from Ayodhya to Gujarat were killed in a fire engulfing the compartment of the train they were traveling in. Later investigations suggested that the fire might have originated from a malfunctioning cooking-gas cylinder. The Hindu right blamed it on Muslims, some of whom had quarreled with the *kar sevaks* at the railway station just before the fire erupted. Modi, who had recently become chief minister of Gujarat, was accused of unleashing a series of riots in the state where nearly 800 Muslims were killed and 150,000 displaced.

In 2014, Modi, proudly flaunting this record of anti-Muslim violence, won the BJP the national elections and became prime minister. A second, even more emphatic, victory in 2019 was anointed by India's Supreme Court in November with a judgment that gave the government the go-ahead for the building of the Ram temple.

On August 5, 2020, while the coronavirus raged unchecked in India, Modi, dressed in shiny, flowing clothes and a white KN95 mask, carried out a long ceremony inaugurating the construction of the temple. While images of Ram and a model of the temple were flashed in front of diaspora supporters gathered in front of a giant screen in Times Square, Modi offered prayers to the Ram idol and the 88-pound silver brick that will serve as the keystone of the foundation. Addressing a subsequent gathering of Hindu-right grandees, many of them dressed in the distinctive saffron that is meant to mark the detachment of the Hindu ascetic from all worldly affairs, Modi did not forget to mention that along with Hindu pride and assertion, the temple would also bring massive economic development to the region.

The one area in which Ayodhya does seem to have grown is as a pilgrimage destination for rural pilgrims who are directed with casual brutality through metal barricades by armed policemen in khaki. Past shops selling sweets and flowers the pilgrims went, hustled by ravenous-looking men offering to be guides, past the competing shrines of dueling monasteries, the most prominent of them the steep, fortresslike shrine of Hanumangarhi that sits on the outer perimeter of Ramkot, the mythical fort of Ram. Beyond, behind more barricades and guarded by more armed police, lay the disputed center where the new temple was being constructed.

Had a great Hindu temple to Ram ever previously existed here? The claim is a surprisingly recent one. In 1990, B. B. Lal, an archaeologist who had conducted digs around the mosque in the mid-'70s and reported little of significance, suddenly claimed in a Hindu-right magazine that his excavations had revealed temple pillars predating the mosque. Lal went on to have a fruitful post-retirement career, publishing ever more speculative books asserting that Ram was a historical person, and receiving two of the highest civilian awards in India from the BJP government in 2000 and 2021.

In 2003, another dig, ordered by the courts, began on the site of the demolished mosque. The dig was carried out by the Archaeological Survey of India (ASI), a state body that reported to the BJP-led government in Delhi. Khalid Ahmad Khan, a septuagenarian who had been a member of the Muslim alliance opposing Hindu claims on the land, had described the dig to me in his house the previous day. Khan had been present as an observer on behalf of the Muslim petitioners, the court-appointed arrangements displaying a portentous attention to balanced representation; 33 percent of the fifty-one-member team from the ASI had been Muslim, with the same proportion of Muslim labor chosen for the actual digging. The 2003 dig, according to the report eventually filed by the ASI, uncovered material going back as far as the thirteenth century BCE, including "glazed pottery, tiles and bones." But the ASI's main contention was that "a massive structure" existed at the site "from the 10th century" CE, on top of which the sixteenth-century mosque had been built, and that the "remains" recovered of this tenth-century structure contained "distinctive features found associated with the temples of North India."

Khan did not believe that the found material provided evidence of a Hindu site, as opposed to a Buddhist or Islamic one. Surrounded by voluminous files of legal documents and newspaper clippings, he gave the impression of clinging to the illusion of democracy and constitutional principles against an ever-encroaching reality. Anxious to assert his loyalty to India and his cordial relations with the Hindu religious leaders, Khan told me that the Hindu argument had been based entirely on faith and belief. The Muslims, however, had depended on evidence. "We produced revenue records, government affidavits, and artifacts. They said their records had been destroyed. I was there during the digging. They found no proof."

Vineet Maurya, another opponent of the temple whom I had met in my hotel, was also skeptical of the Hindu temple theory. Maurya, who converted in his youth from Hinduism to Buddhism, was engaged in a legal dispute with the government about its forcible acquisition of his family home in Ayodhya as part of its expanded temple complex. Maurya, who came from a family of agricultural laborers, had belonged to one of the castes at the bottom of the hierarchy. His break with Hinduism had been accompanied by a long journey of educating himself. He had a law degree, was learning Pali so he could read Buddhist texts, and was studying for a master's degree in ancient history from Awadh University. He believed that the oldest civilizational artifacts discovered at the site were Buddhist rather than Hindu, and as such the site should be turned into a "national monument" that brought in tourists and pilgrims interested in India's Buddhist past.

Given that the area in the sixth century BCE had been a Buddhist center of some repute called Saket, it is quite likely that a Buddhist structure had indeed existed on the site. It could also be that a Hindu temple was later established on the site as Buddhism was pushed out of India. But this temple would not be older than the tenth or eleventh century CE, and would have featured, according to the ASI's own report, gods and goddesses other than Ram. Except in the Hindu right's colorful murals and popular television skits, no one seems to know quite what happened between the tenth and the sixteenth centuries, when the Babri Masjid came up. It is quite possible, for instance, that the large mosque was built on top of a smaller Islamic place of worship, which could indeed have been built on a Hindu temple built on top of a Buddhist structure.

The ASI report itself had noted defensively of its "evidence" that its work had been done hurriedly and under difficult circumstances, including heightened security checks, torrential monsoon rains, and monkeys who made a mockery of the court's directions to preserve materials "under lock and seal." The Supreme Court judgment in 2019 that granted the site to Hindus spent an enormous length of time going over the arguments and counterarguments of the ASI report. The judgment, in keeping with the verbose nature of the Indian judiciary, is over a thousand pages long, filled with floral asides that bring in comparisons to ships and corporations to decide if Ram can be considered a "legal personality," with gratuitous references to Wordsworth, Karl Popper, and the "distinguished archaeologist, Sir Mortimer Wheeler."

As significant as the verbal excess of the judgment might be its extratextual aspects. The five-judge bench delivering it was headed by Ranjan Gogoi, who had been appointed as chief justice of the Supreme Court under the Modi government a little over a year earlier, in October 2018. Hounded by accusations of sexual harassment and persecution by a junior employee, Gogoi went on to deliver a series of controversial verdicts in favor of the Modi government, including the removal of a special provision for the Muslim majority in Kashmir and the creation of a register that targeted Muslims in Assam and stripped at least a million of them of their Indian citizenship. Eight days after delivering the Ayodhya judgment, Gogoi retired from the Supreme Court. Within four months of his retirement, he was nominated to the

Rajya Sabha—one of the two houses of the Indian legislature—by Modi's government.

"There is no specific finding that the underlying structure was a temple dedicated to Lord Ram," the Supreme Court judgment conceded. It also agreed that the demolition of the mosque had been illegal and that the Ram idol had been smuggled illegally into the site in 1949. Nevertheless, on the basis of "documentary and oral evidence," it decided, in tortuous prose, that the "faith and belief of Hindus since prior to construction of Mosque and subsequent thereto has always been that Janmaasthan of Lord Ram is the place where Babri Mosque has been constructed which faith and belief is proved." It ordered the site to be handed over for the building of the temple, while an alternative location, on the outskirts of the town on the highway to Lucknow, was to be given to Muslims for a new mosque, to replace the one that had been destroyed.

§

One afternoon, I went to meet Dr. Anil at his copy shop. We were planning to travel to Karsevakpuram, the Ayodhya neighborhood that has gone from being a temporary encampment for *kar sevaks* in the '90s to becoming a permanent feature of the town. But elections for the Uttar Pradesh legislature were to take place in February 2022—which the BJP would go on to win on March 11—and Dr. Anil needed me to wait until a television crew had arrived to interview him. We waited in the shop, a cubicle dominated by a photocopy machine and a desk holding a computer and printer. Generous cracks ran across the unpainted floor, dust sat on open shelves built into the wall, and brown plastic stools served as chairs, the brand name stickers still attached.

When the television crew arrived, we stepped out and went over to the edge of the highway. The name of the channel, according to the burly, bearded producer, was Newsprint. It wasn't a joke. He was earnest, maybe slightly evasive as he told me the channel was based in Delhi and uploaded directly onto YouTube. I wondered if it was part of the Hindu right's fecund disinformation network of talk shows, trolls, and WhatsApp groups, and if the intention behind filming outside was to create as much of a public spectacle as possible. Later, when I searched for the channel on YouTube, I couldn't find it. In the moment though, the afternoon sun beating down on the television crew and its subjects, the interview seemed both elaborately contrived and deeply revealing of conditions in Ayodhya.

The BJP was seeking reelection in the place that had changed its political fortunes, where a utopia once existed, where—according to a pamphlet widely available in Ayodhya—virtuous Hindu men and women lived in sky-high mansions where the floors were heaped with gems. I took a look at my surroundings. Across from me, the Buddhist-inspired domes of Ram Manohar Lohia University offered a faint reminder of other histories of the region. And yet all pasts seemed irrelevant against the distressing reality of the present.

A billboard hemmed in by electric wires and hung crookedly from a tree looked down at the crew. The most prominent of the faces displayed on it were that of Modi and Yogi Adityanath, the shaven-headed, saffron-clad Hindu monk who is chief minister of the state and whose reputation for instigating anti-Muslim violence rivals that of Modi's. The long years of their combined rule had not produced much: a newish sidewalk already cracked and smeared with garbage and cow shit; small, crammed shops similar to Dr. Anil's; and bright, garish advertisements for banks, mobile phones, and tutoring agencies that promised a pathway to a government job. Over 40 percent of the population in the district is illiterate; nearly 40 percent lives below the poverty line.

None of this appeared to have any purchase on the interview that unfolded, the knot of people around the camera caught in billowing dust and exhaust from passing vehicles. The gathering was still small, but there was a practiced TikTok flourish to the young reporter as he began, twisting his body into a V and pivoting on his sandals as he held the mic in one hand and gestured with his other at the people gathered around. First in line was Dr. Anil, confident in his pronouncements. He was followed by a man called Haji Syed Ahmed, a member of the Muslim wing headed by Dr. Anil. Ahmed, too, spoke in sound bites, confident of the good work being done by the Hindu right, although the most distinctive thing about him was his elegance in that crowd of slovenly Hindu men. He wore a long gray *kurta*, white pajamas, and stylish blue sneakers. His neatly trimmed beard, his white skullcap, and blue checkered keffiyeh indicated his status as a devout Muslim, as did the adjective "Haji" before his name. Earlier, he had told me a convoluted story about his shop being forcefully occupied by another man with political connections and his hopes that the Hindu right would be able to get it back for him. He was, he admitted sorrowfully, more or less ostracized by other Muslims for his overt support of the Hindu right. There were others Dr. Anil had summoned to give their views, including a Muslim woman in a hijab who was distracted from the interview by her restless toddler children.

The lovefest for Modi and Yogi looked like it would go on forever, but two passersby decided to intervene. Both men appeared to be supporters of the SP, confident and articulate in spite of being vastly outnumbered. The BJP's cow protection laws had resulted in feral cattle running wild and destroying crops in the fields, one of the men shouted. His companion, younger, more cerebral, responded to his hecklers with verve, talking about the corruption of the Hindu-right politicians whose names could be found in the Paradise Papers, the huge leak of financial documents in November 2017 that revealed the offshore banking accounts of multinational corporations and the global elite. The reporter got increasingly flustered, as did Dr. Anil. At the university across, classes had ended, and students slowed down on their way home to listen. A few were women, but they did not linger long. The Muslim woman had departed with her children, without speaking, and it was almost entirely a male crowd gathered now around the television crew.

Although it was all talk, there was a physicality to the scene, the height and burliness of the Yadav men offering a challenge that could not easily be quashed. The crowd got larger and louder, and small, independent quarrels began to break out on the edges, Dr. Anil struggling to be heard above the noise as he faced the camera once again. Another big man entered the scene, his political affiliation obvious from his Brahmin's topknot. I got the impression that he had been summoned there to wrest the initiative back, which he did by ignoring all questions from the reporter and raising his voice in a chant. It was the war cry of the Hindu right coming out of his mouth, the same one that had resounded in the air the day the Babri Masjid was demolished, the same one that Muslims hear when pogroms break out, that clogs the television channels and social media networks in India as prelude or punctuation to a vitriolic outpouring of abuse. "Jai Shri Ram!" he shouted, and "Jai Shri Ram," the crowd responded, tentatively at first and then louder by the moment. The Yadav men laughed, shook their heads disbelievingly, and exited the scene.

§

Another billboard featuring the Modi-Yogi combine graced the entrance to the site where the bricks gathered in the nineties are kept. It was hard to believe that these were the *shilas* gathered from all over India and abroad, blessed by priests in Sanskrit and trucked to Ayodhya in ceremonial processions of *kar sevaks* displaying unsheathed swords. The place had the feel of a storage shed, with waterlogged ground crisscrossed by policemen changing shifts, elderly *kar sevaks* in saffron *dhotis* going out for evening walks, and monkeys foraging for food. The bricks were stacked in untidy columns against the walls, along with elaborately carved columns that seemed to belong to some forgotten 1.0 version of the Ram temple.

Promises had been made that the bricks would be used for the temple being constructed, but it seemed unlikely that more than a few would find their way there. And yet what else was the entire project of Ramrajya other than endless symbolism evoked to obscure tawdry reality? A temple stood in the center of the yard, but it was not the temple that caught the eye as much as the murals decorating its outer wall. History had been turned there into a singular story of the oppression visited upon Hindus and their courageous resistance: cruel-looking men in vaguely Arab outfits brandished swords and fired cannons at the temple supposedly torn down to make way for the Babri Masjid; next to them, the Sikh reformer Govind Singh was busy fighting on horseback, a deft touch meant to draw the Sikhs into the Hindu-right project; below, the faces of two brothers from Kolkata killed in the police firing of 1991 looked out, the calm resolution of their faces borrowed from iconic representations of Indian anti-colonial revolutionaries.

Karsevakpuram itself was different, the symbolism held in check for the quieter machinations of power. It housed the offices of the VHP, which had fronted the assault on the mosque. Armed sentries were on duty around the large complex, neat and quiet, with flowers and well-watered lawns. It was the first time since I had been in Ayodhya that I felt a sense of order, and with it came the sensation of being in close proximity to authority.

§

Fifteen Hindu men comprise the committee in charge of the construction of the temple, which is already mired in controversy. A vast amount of the money donated for construction—there are pictures of Modi soliciting money for the temple throughout banks in India—is said to have been siphoned off. Land near the temple had allegedly been acquired by a close relative of a senior BJP functionary and then flipped over to the temple trust at many times the purchase price. A member of the temple trust committee had also apparently rented out offices to Larsen & Toubro, the Indian engineering firm—the name harks back to the Danish men who started the original, colonial-era company—constructing the temple pro bono.

I had tried talking to this member. His name was Dr. Anil Mishra, the "Dr." in this case referring to his homeopathic practice. Mishra, who had apparently installed an elevator inside his multistory home to signal his newly acquired affluence, sounded alarmed when I called him. I should talk to his colleague Champat Rai, general secretary of the temple trust committee, he said. He himself was unable to tell me anything. I was unsurprised by Mishra's refusal to talk to the media. The Hindu right, which refers to journalists as "presstitutes," is choosy about who it grants access to and what it reveals. But Dr. Anil—the original one—was confident that he could introduce me to Rai, and so we loitered inside Karsevakpuram, the quiet of the evening occasionally interrupted by monkeys jumping from rooftop to rooftop.

A convoy swept in, white SUVs disgorging men in crisp white clothes, the policemen and hangers-on attentive. Dr. Anil suddenly appeared diminished, but I could also see something of his determination as he attached himself to the men striding into the main office, introducing first himself and then me. I could sense the shimmering outline of a system built entirely on patronage and influence and that Dr. Anil's stock had perhaps risen subtly because, in spite of his modest motorcycle, his failing copy shop, and his truncated position at the university, he had brought a journalist from the United States with him to this place.

Inside the office, Rai listened to my request for an interview, his smooth, clean-shaven face animated by something that could have been suspicion, or fatigue, or both. An Indian man wearing jeans was introduced to me as a North American working for the Hindu cause. We made small talk about New York. "I have no time for you today," Rai said finally. "But tomorrow, I can give you fifteen minutes. Come here at 5 p.m."

The next evening, I waited for nearly an hour at Karsevakpuram. Neither Rai nor any of his entourage showed up. Instead, I found myself chatting with a man called Hazari Lal who sold incense and ayurvedic medicine at an exhibition hall near the front gate. A giant model of the Ram temple sat under bright fluorescent lights, beige rather than the ocher chosen for the version under construction. A large photograph of Ashok Singhal, the VHP president at the time of the demolition, squatted in front of the model, the base of the temple cluttered with random slabs of marble and what I assumed were consecrated *shilas*. Paint had flaked off in patches from the yellow guard rail around the model and the pink walls of the hall. A raised relief map of the temple site occupied the outer perimeter of the model; apart from a few yellow blocks indicating buildings, the rest was unpainted concrete, as if the maker had become exhausted halfway through the project.

Lal, insisting that I sit with him, brought plastic chairs out into the open so that we would see Rai if he showed up. Lal had been a *kar sevak* during the attempt to storm the Babri Masjid in 1990. Two years later, he returned for the successful assault on the mosque. He described climbing up to one of the domes and falling from it, injuring his head and fracturing his left hand. He had been imprisoned for two weeks for his part in the demolition and then released on bail. Beyond that, there had been no legal repercussions for his actions.

There was no guilt, no self-consciousness, in Lal's telling of the story. The mosque and Muslims were a foreign imposition to him, and his world, apart from that spectacular outburst in the early '90s, appeared to have been largely side-stepped by modernity. Although only in his early sixties, he gave the impression of being an old man, aged according to the calendar of impoverishment that holds sway over so much of life in this part of India. There were hints of personal tragedy, of a son who worked in a factory and whose little girl had died. When he posed for a picture for me or took out an old mobile phone to ask me to enter my number on its tiny keypad, I got the sense of a man mimicking what he had seen others around him do, which is probably why in spite of his violent past as a *kar sevak* and his proximity to power, he evoked mostly vulnerability. His right eye was opaque with a cataract. I recalled how the previous day, he had asked Dr. Anil if he could help him find a clinic where the eye could be checked out. Dr. Anil had been pleasant but noncommittal. Later, he had compared Lal to Rai. "Some have the capacity to rise, others don't," he had confided to me. "That is the only difference between men."

§

One morning, as I made my way into the heart of Ayodhya with Dr. Anil, we bought *pedas*—round, hard discs of sweet cream that look like cheese—as an offering from a sweet shop owned by one of Dr. Anil's Hindu-right colleagues. We left our slippers there for safekeeping as well; our phones and wallets we had already given to the driver of the car, waiting in a parking lot on the edge of the pilgrimage zone. It was early but already crowded, the pilgrims clustered in front of Hanumangarhi, where three streets converge in a blur of noise and color.

The ground was slimy under our feet as we climbed up to the shrine of Hanuman, the monkey god. A beloved, all-action figure in the *Ramayana*, where he is Ram's most devoted ally, Hanuman too has morphed in recent years into an icon of violent Hindu masculinity. He is now visible everywhere, particularly on motorcycle windscreens and the rear windows of cars, as "Angry Hanuman," a contorted face in saffron and black that went viral after Modi praised the design at an election rally in 2018.

Modi, accompanied by Yogi and trailed by bodyguards and a television crew, had visited the Hanumangarhi shrine in August 2020 after the Ram temple ceremony. He had used an alternative entrance, one that allowed him to avoid the climb. The shrine had been emptied out for him, and he had stood directly in front of the Hanuman idol, swirling a lit lamp and muttering a prayer.

We had no such luck. We climbed the 200 steps, on top of which a sign announced "Only Hindus May Enter." In front, a crowd jostled to get closer to the shrine, priests leaning down from the inner sanctorum to accept their offerings. Dr. Anil led me into the press of bodies and glided away. I stood there amid the crush of bodies, uncertain of what to do. I could barely make out the features of the Hanuman deity. Later, when watching Modi's visit on YouTube, I would get a sense of it, diminutive and aniconic, a far cry from Angry Hanuman. I held my bag of *pedas* up, found a priest willing to receive it, and then I was out of the crush, relieved.

Dr. Anil looked at me with surprise. "What did you do with the *pedas*?" he asked. He stared at me with astonishment when he heard that I'd given them to the priest but not taken them back, as I apparently should have. When I first met Dr. Anil, all I had told him was that I was a journalist based in New York writing a story on the Ram temple. Dr. Anil had come to the conclusion that I was a devout, right-wing Hindu all on his own. Now I could sense a hesitation, as if he was considering for the first time who I might really be. Standing with my back to the crowd, I felt a wave of unease. Just the day before, the *Guardian* had published a piece of mine on the Modi government's practice of planting malware on the computers of activists and incarcerating them for years without trial under an anti-terror law.

But the moment passed. Dr. Anil, happy to have a chance to laugh at me, decided that I was merely displaying the ignorance of someone not born in the Hindu heartland. We went into the office area to try and find the head priest, a man whose Persian title of *Gadd-e-nashin*—Keeper of the seat—indicated the origins of Hanumangarhi in the time of Muslim kings. The *Gadd-e-nashin* was not in, however, and Dr. Anil led me to another priest, a gigantic man who sat on an open platform meeting devotees. I went through the motion of seeking his blessing, which he granted perfunctorily, tossing some flowers in my direction while waving a white, ceremonial whisk with the other.

Although Dr. Anil seemed inclined to introduce me to one senior priest after another, I persuaded him out of Hanumangarhi. In front of us lay the site of the future temple and the temporary shrine housing the Ram idol. Dr. Anil was disappointed that we were approaching it from the commoners' entrance rather than through the VIP access route that allowed important people to drive right up to the gate and avoid the crowds. Instead, we waited in front of the security booth in a long, straggling line, exposed to marauding monkeys and touts hustling people to leave their belongings in lockers available at nearby shops. At Hanumangarhi, the pilgrims had been mostly poor and local, many of them women and the elderly. Now I began to spot urban, middle-class men who had come from southern India and Kolkata.

Through the security booth we went, stepping into a corridor enclosed above and to the sides by wired netting, like a bunker from which to monitor the position of an opposing army. An excitement animated the crowd as we progressed through the labyrinthine corridor, accompanied by the shouts of policemen asking everyone to keep moving.

Everyone slowed down again as we approached the temporary shrine. The idol was set well back from the pilgrims sequestered in the iron corridor, attendant priests handing out packets of consecrated sweets through an opening in the wired netting. I lingered as long as I could. After the decades of violence in the name of Ram, portrayed in memes as a muscular Uberman, all veiny biceps and chiseled six-packs, the appearance of the idol, small, dark-skinned, and with big manga eyes, was unexpected. Because this was Ram's birthplace, the idol was of an infant Ram—Ram Lalla—and just a little over six inches tall.

This was the god who had changed the fortunes of a nation. He had been smuggled in under the cover of darkness, in 1949, and hurried out amid the noise of a mosque being brought down, in 1990, a god placed here and there by his followers. Now, he looked like a doll sitting in a temporary dollhouse in front of a bunker inside a fortress. We had just seen the site of his future temple, marked by yellow earth movers stranded in the vastness of an empty square.

§

Not long after my visit to the temple site, I went to meet Dinendra Das, a member of the temple trust committee. Das is the *mahant*—head—of the Nirmohi *akhara*, a powerful religious order that owns temples and monasteries in a number of states in North India. It is one of the claimants to the disputed site in Ayodhya, but it has been sidelined by the Supreme Court's decision that the Ram idol will be represented on earth by representatives of the VHP. Das's presence on the committee seemed to reflect the compromise worked out by the Hindu right, where politicos like Rai and Mishra called the shots while the priests were kept onboard in symbolic positions.

I had been told that Das and his *akhara* were disgruntled with their secondary role, but Das revealed nothing of this discontent when I met him in his monastery. With his saffron garb and flowing gray hair and beard, he was far more personable in real life than the cross-eyed photo of his displayed on the temple trust website. It was obvious that his position on the committee, along with his status as an important religious leader, had brought some perks into his life. An official car was parked in the yard for his use, complete with government license plate and VIP lights. A personal bodyguard, a policeman in plainclothes, stayed present throughout my conversation with him.

Yet there was also a difference between him and power brokers like Rai as well as with aspirants to power like Dr. Anil. Das was far more awkward, flattered that a journalist from New York had arrived to interview him. There was something appealing about the transparency of his vanity, the way he adjusted his clothes when it was time for a photograph or the manner in which he conveyed to me that his favorite subjects as a college student had been English, economics, and Sanskrit. His original name had been Dinendra Kumar Pandey. Like all monks, he was required to dispense with his caste name and take on a common last name used by everyone. He became Dinendra Das in 1992, when he took his vows. In 2017, he became the *mahant*.

The wealth, ambition, and aspiration that the Ram temple had precipitated all around was more intermittent in its presence in the Nirmohi *akhara*. The *mahant*'s room was big and airy; the floor had been tiled recently and the ductless air conditioner on the wall was new and sleek. They were planning to rebuild the two other structures in the complex, grassy and overgrown, set back from one of the narrow lanes curling through Ayodhya. One building would be converted into a guest house for visiting devotees and monks. The other would be torn down for a new complex where the shrine would face outward, toward the road, in a concession to modern sensibilities that require even a deity to advertise its presence.

But if change was coming, indeed had already come, it had not yet made its full impact on the *akhara*. I was invited to lunch with the monks—the *mahant* ate separately—in the main building. It was in the old North Indian *haveli* style, with an inner courtyard around which the shrine and the quarters of the monks were arranged. The deity faced into this courtyard, and I was led past it by monks in their early teens who looked at me with curiosity. The kitchen was narrow, with old, high ceilings. The meal consisted of rotis and rice with dal and a vegetable curry.

We ate sitting on the floor, served by a muscular monk with a Brahmin's topknot and a wicked sense of humor. When I apologized and said I hoped that they had not been waiting because of me—the interview with the *mahant* had gone on beyond their lunch hour—he replied, "You're exactly the reason we've all been waiting with empty bellies." There was no malice in the comment. When I later asked the assembled monks, ranging from the teenage boys to men in their seventies, how they had been affected by the coronavirus, the same man responded. "We've all come here to die," he said, referring to the belief that by cutting off ties to family and the material world and living out their years on sacred ground, they had the opportunity to break the cycle of rebirth. "But god has a way of not giving people what they want," he chuckled. "So those who want to live are dying, and those of us who want to die are living."

I found his humor refreshing, displaying perhaps an awareness that lives, religious as well as secular, are built in part on fantasy. That had been apparent when I asked the *mahant* about the daily routine of the Ram Lalla idol. The *mahant* had been bemused by my question, but not annoyed. It had taken him a few phone calls to determine the exact details. The infant Ram was woken at five in the morning, I was told. He was bathed and then offered *aarti*, a ritual in which an open flame is waved to accompanying songs, the first of five such *aarti* sessions punctuating his day. From 7 to 11, devotees came to visit Ram Lalla. He ate at 11:30, took a nap, and was woken again at 1:30 for a second round of visitors. At 6:50, he had a substantial dinner of *puris*, *sabzi*, and *kheer*. At 7:30, after a final dose of *aarti*, he was put to sleep and the shrine shut down for the night. Two bodyguards were always present, in eight-hour shifts, but they were not allowed to carry weapons.

There was something odd but endearing about a monastic order of childless men ostensibly devoted to taking care of a never-changing, never-growing infant. But these rituals of care were a long way from the Hindu masculinity I had seen in evidence all over Ayodhya. Khan, the Muslim opponent of the temple, had told me with some sadness that the Hindu right did not really believe that Ram was a god. "The temple is not being built to Ram the god but to Ram the ideal man, what they call 'Purushottam Ram,'" he had said. This was certainly how Dr. Anil had referred to him. "Ram is not a common man. As a son, brother, cousin, his character is that of 'Maryada Purushottam,'" he had told me on our first meeting. "Why do institutions today fail?" Dr. Anil had continued. "Why do we have murders and rapes? The writers of the constitution forgot our past. The constitution brings things from the outside. In Ram's time, there were no locks in houses, no gates in temples. This temple will start that culture of Ram."

And yet Ram the ideal son, brother, and king is a long way from the versions of him encountered in the many adaptations of the *Ramayana* that flowered in the Indian subcontinent and beyond through the centuries. Although he is the seventh avatar of Vishnu, and in that sense immortal, Ram doesn't always remember his divine antecedents. Often, he struggles with events and actions and their consequences, and his life is, from one perspective, utterly tragic. Banished from Ayodhya because his father wants to appease his younger wife—Ram's stepmother—who wants her biological son to inherit the throne, Ram is unable to prevent the abduction of his wife Sita while in exile. When he wins her back, after an epic war that involves the help of Hanuman and other monkeys, he is hounded by the suspicions of his conservative subjects that Sita has not remained faithful to him while in captivity. Even a fire test of purity by Sita cannot stop the tongues wagging, and Ram banishes a pregnant Sita to the forests. All this is the backdrop to his utopian rule. Even his death has a tinge of darkness to it, with Ram—at least in some versions—finally drowning himself in the river.

It is possible to argue that this very frailty and conflict in Ram endeared him to the spiritual traditions that rose around him. Often, the stories and songs composed and sung about him came from marginalized sections, from men of the weaver caste, like Kabir, and from women like Mirabai, people removed from direct access to wealth, power, and knowledge. But these approaches to Ram are a long way from the toxic version on display in Ayodhya and in India at large, a version that always tends toward Purushottam Ram.

I recalled how Dr. Anil, after the visit to the temple site, had been in a gregarious mood that appeared to have nothing to do with his having visited Ram Lalla. As we walked back past shops selling religious souvenirs, saffron scarves featuring the Angry Hanuman prominent among them, the conversation had turned, somehow, to Muslims. "They had their chance in 1947," he said. "They wanted a separate Muslim nation and they got it. Why do they still stay on here?" They were mostly Hindus who had long ago converted to Islam. To stay on in India, they should reconvert, he believed. What if they wanted to be in India as Muslims? I asked. He shrugged. "What can we do? We can't kill them," he said. They should have their voting rights and any state benefits taken away, he believed. They could live and work in India, but no more. It was a horrifying vision, one that has already been put into place in Assam and was the other part of the culture of Ram that the temple would bring into being.

Earlier in the day, just before we visited the Ram idol, Dr. Anil had wanted me to stop by at an apartment he had bought as an investment. It was close to the center of Ayodhya, and he described to me how everything would be transformed once the temple was complete. The riverbank littered with cattle sheds and cowshit would be converted into a promenade. Condominiums would come up everywhere, as would a new airport being constructed not far from his photocopying business. Devotees with dollars in their bank accounts would be whisked from Delhi to Ayodhya by air or a high-speed train. They would relax in luxury, seven-star hotels on the outskirts of the town and be driven along wide highways directly to the new Ram temple. The website for the temple offered additional details. Visitors would be able to enjoy a "special peace zone for deeper meditation," gaze at a

"Lily-pond [sic] and Musical Fountains," and check out the VIP cousins of the cattle I had seen everywhere being pampered at the "Adarsh Goshala" shelter for cows.

The highways existed—I had been on them. But Dr. Anil's apartment was at the end of a grim block of concrete—housing bearing the unmistakable stamp of being built for the lower middle class by a government agency, much like the one my parents and I had occupied in Kolkata in the nineties. There were cars parked in front of the two-story buildings in a demonstration of the upward mobility that had come to Ayodhya. But the electric wires ran in manic fashion from rusting, crooked poles, the paint had peeled off the walls, and mildew grew like an alien infestation on the window ledges. Dr. Anil led me to his second-floor apartment, empty, still in the process of being finished. He spent a long time washing the stainless steel sink. Then he showed me the squat toilet, which he said had been relocated at considerable expense because it originally pointed in a direction considered wrong by the scriptures. Everything about the apartment and its surroundings was miserable, but Dr. Anil's energy and optimism seemed boundless.

I could understand why. Ayodhya, after all, is only the start of the liberation the Hindu right envisions for India. In Varanasi—a city far older and much more central to Hindu traditions than Ayodhya—the Gyan Vapi mosque sits surrounded by barricades and policemen while the Shiva temple next door is expanded along lines similar to what is being done with the new Ram temple. There are demands to install an idol inside a mosque in the town of Mathura because it supposedly occupies the birthplace of Krishna, another avatar of Vishnu. There is even talk that the Taj Mahal is really an ancient Shiva temple appropriated by Muslims that must be returned to its former glory. The Ram temple coming up in Ayodhya, built with stone from Rajasthan, designed by an architect from Gujarat, and funded by dollars from the diaspora in the West, is only the beginning of an effort to construct a past that never was, in the hope of devising a future from which India's Muslim inhabitants can be erased.

Chapter 6
Impossible Machines

Vimanas and Hindu-Right Fantasies
of Ancient Technology

On January 4, at the annual Indian Science Congress in Mumbai, Anand Bodas, a former principal of a pilot-training academy, and a professor named Ameya Jadhav presented a joint paper titled "Ancient Indian Aviation Technology."*

The Congress, a prestigious event that dates to 1914, included programs on advances ranging from India's recent Mars orbital mission to developments in cancer biology, with talks by Indian and foreign scientists, among them a number of Nobel laureates. The paper by Bodas and Jadhav was part of a symposium on "Ancient Sciences Through Sanskrit," a series of presentations on the technical knowledge in old Indian texts, usually understood to be considerable, especially when it comes to mathematics, metallurgy, and medicine. But "Ancient Indian Aviation Technology" had run into trouble even before the Congress began, when Ramprasad Gandhiraman, an Indian materials scientist affiliated with NASA, started an online petition on Change.org against its "pseudo-science." The campaign, which garnered 1,600 supporters, cited a

---

* First published in the *New Republic*, June 2015.

report in the newspaper *Mumbai Mirror* in which Bodas had said that his paper was based on an ancient Indian treatise that had been forgotten because of "the passage of time, foreign rulers ruling us, and things being stolen from this country."

Despite Gandhiraman's campaign, the paper was presented as planned. In clips run throughout India's media channels, Bodas can be seen gently declaiming, from behind a full white beard and an upturned mustache, "Aeroplane is a vehicle which travels through the air from one country to another country, from one continent to another continent, and from one planet to another planet." Although neither Bodas nor the organizers were willing to share the paper with the media, the numerous reports on it, as well the abstract, which is available, give a fairly clear idea of what else he had to say (his collaborator Jadhav seems largely absent apart from being listed as coauthor). "Ancient Sanskrit literature is full of descriptions of flying machines—*Vimanas*," the abstract says. These *vimanas*, according to Bodas, had been developed anywhere from 7,000 to 9,000 years ago.

Bodas's claim about *vimanas* is only one in a series of recent pronouncements about the technological marvels of ancient India. Since the Bharatiya Janata Party (BJP), led by the Prime Minister Modi, won the national elections last year, it has become increasingly commonplace to make fantastic references to ancient India, a time when seemingly everything from televisions to nuclear weapons existed. This glorious past tends to be elastic in its timeline but in general refers to a stretch running from around 1500 BCE to 300 CE. This marks the birth of Sanskrit, the Indo-European language of pastoralist nomads who settled in northern India and who composed the central religious and poetic texts—including the Vedas—of what later came to be called Hinduism. As the Vedic culture spread deeper into the Indian subcontinent, giving rise to monarchies and republics, it produced much in the way of philosophy, poetry, and religion, interacting with Greek, Arab, Chinese, and indigenous cultures. There were substantial critiques of the Vedic texts along with the texts themselves, Buddhism emerging from the most influential of these, and significant achievements in the fields of mathematics, medicine, and astronomy.

For the contemporary Hindu right, however—the BJP and its supporters—ancient India is a far less complex place. It is seen as a time of pure Hinduism, created by Sanskrit-speaking people who had always lived on the Indian subcontinent, with a unified, homogeneous religion and culture free of the foreign presence to come in later centuries, especially with the arrival of Islam and then the West in India. In this paradisiacal ancient India, the Hindu right finds evidence of a wide array of modern devices and technologies. Modi himself, when inaugurating a hospital last October, added genetic engineering and plastic surgery to the list. "We worship Ganeshji," he said, referring to the elephant-headed god. "Some plastic surgeon must have been around at that time, who by attaching an elephant head to the body of a human started off plastic surgery."

But what comes up often, in newly introduced school textbooks and in comments made by Y. Sudershan Rao, the man the BJP recently appointed to head the Indian Council of Historical Research, are the *vimanas*, or Vedic aircraft. Capable of interplanetary travel and invisibility, possessing radar systems and mine detectors, they capture the imagination of this resurgent, neo-Hindu India like nothing else.

The ancient Indian treatise mentioned in Bodas's paper, forgotten because of the passage of time and the cultural amnesia injected into India by foreigners ruling the country, is the *Vymanika Shastra*, or "Science of Aeronautics." Supposedly part of a larger work now lost to us called *Yantra Sarvasva*, or "All About Machines," the *VS* is the canonical text referred to in all the discussion of Vedic *vimanas*. It also happens to be, from another, more literal, perspective, a work just about a century old.

The person credited as the author of the *VS* is a Hindu guru from the Vedic age known as Maharshi Bhardwaj. The memorization of Sanskrit texts and their oral transmission through generations is a feature of the Vedic era, with emphasis on retaining the content of the canonical works unchanged while allowing for variation and reinvention with imaginative genres such as epics. But the *VS*, in contrast to other Vedic works, never appears until the late nineteenth or early twentieth century. A guru, whose name is not known and who had received Bhardwaj's wisdom from generations of sages transmitting it through a secret oral tradition (or who was given the text directly by a divine source), "revealed" the *VS* to a young Brahmin named Subbaraya Sastry.

Sastry appears to have been a poor man born in a village in southern India, married at the age of eight, and reduced to begging in order to support a large family. An attack of smallpox killed some of his siblings and crippled him. Sastry took to wandering the countryside, living on grass and leaves, until he met the unnamed guru, who was possessed of mystical healing powers and who also apparently contained in his memory the millennia-old *VS* and other Vedic texts.

After curing Sastry of his ailment, the guru recited the *VS* to him in a cave. Subsequently, Sastry, after he had returned home and settled down, developed a reputation of his own as a mystic, given to dictating portions of the *VS* to his followers. This process, which occurred between 1900 and 1922, eventually led to the full Sanskrit text of the *VS* being written down, with copies of the manuscript apparently placed with his disciples and in libraries. Sastry even commissioned drawings of the *vimanas* mentioned in the text from T. K. Ellappa, a draftsman who had studied at an engineering college.

Impossible Machines

This literary biography is, admittedly, a conjecture created by a group of scientists studying the *VS* in the mid-'70s. Not only does the *VS* have no written point of origin until the early twentieth century, it announces itself to the world at large only in independent India, trailing the story of its complex, mystical origins behind it, but without any verifiable sources. Its existence was first noted in 1952 in the southern city of Mysore by G. R. Josyer, the founder of an organization called the International Academy of Sanskrit Research. By this time, Sastry was no longer alive. Josyer claimed, in an interview with the Press Trust of India, a government news agency, that his newly established academy had collected a number of manuscripts thousands of years old, but which, in spite of their great age, dealt not with "the mysticism of ancient Hindu philosophy" but with "things vital for the existence of man and [the] progress of nations both in times of peace and war." One of these manuscripts, the *VS*, was on aeronautics, with details about the construction of "various types of aircraft for civil aviation and for warfare."

Josyer claimed that the opening portion of the *VS* was handwritten in a small exercise book brought to him by a guest on June 28, 1951, the very day his academy was inaugurated by the maharaja of Mysore. After examining the manuscript and showing it to the maharaja, Josyer gave it back to the anonymous guest, who returned it to Venkatarama Sastry, adopted son of Subbaraya Sastry. Josyer later contacted him and borrowed copies of the manuscript, promising to publish the work.

The interview with the news agency (which may never have taken place; the only record of it appears in Josyer's foreword to the *VS*) was a prelude to that process of publication. It brought him "fan mail," Josyer writes, from air force officials, journalists, Hindu priests, ministers, and civil aviation mandarins. James Burke of *Life International* wrote to ask Josyer if he could see the manuscript. Josyer replied, "Please wire one thousand dollars, and then come." He was more hospitable to Jean Lyon, a journalist from New York. "She came and saw the MSS, and recorded her interview with us in her book *Just Half a World Away*," Josyer wrote, deploying a royal first person plural throughout, "concluding with the charge that we were guilty of a rabid nationalism, seeking to wipe out everything since the Vedas!"

Unfazed by such criticism from foreigners, Josyer published a Sanskrit-Hindi edition in 1959. But he discontinued its printing when he received a "harsh letter" from Venkatarama Sastry, the man who had given him the manuscripts, accusing him of exploiting them for his "personal benefit." Despite that, enthusiastic letters kept coming from India and around the world, Josyer wrote, and he decided to bring out an English translation. "Thus at the age of 81, we had to sit up and translate the technical Sanskrit into readable English, and scrutinize the printing of both the Sanskrit and English, involving the strain of multiple proofreading. The finance required was considerable, and as no help was forthcoming, we had to scrape together the meager savings of a life-time, procure needful printing equipment at mounting costs, engage labor at emergency rates, and at long last, with the help of Divine grace, are able to herald the birth of the volume, which has been in gestation for over ninety years!"

§

The English edition that appeared in 1973 did not quite receive the acclaim Josyer wanted. Lyon, in her account of meeting him in 1952, had written that he had denounced Nehru's "modern" government for being uninterested in the secrets "locked" inside the *VS* "This would put India far ahead of the rest of the world in aeronautics," said Josyer. "The knowledge in this manuscript would make us world leaders. But does our 'modern' government have the vision? ... It would rather ape the West and lag behind it, than follow its own cultural heritage and be leagues ahead of everyone." Josyer's suspicion about his modern fellow Indians may have been right. A year after the publication of the English edition, five scientists from the Indian Institute of Science co-authored an article on the *VS* in the journal *Scientific Opinion*.

The scientists, while remarkably respectful of Sastry's mysticism, saw the *VS* as a creation entirely of his imagination, written in a Sanskrit that was modern in its meter and language rather than Vedic. As for the *vimanas* described in the *VS*, they declared that "on the basis of the principles of geometry, materials, chemistry, and operational data," the text "shows a complete lack of understanding of the dynamics of the flight of heavier-than-air craft." They found verses that violated "Newton's laws," mentioned aircraft speeds of 8,000 miles per hour (which no contemporary craft in their time had attained within the Earth's atmosphere), and instances suggesting the use of electric motors that have existed only since the nineteenth century. In studying the *Rukma Vimana*, a five-tier aircraft with passenger cabins on the third level, they initially thought it to be quite meaningful, operating like a "vertical takeoff and landing craft." Nevertheless, they regretfully concluded, on close scrutiny of text and diagram, that it is a "decided impossibility." While the drawings demonstrate a knowledge of modern machinery, the scientists wrote, the text and the drawings often do not correlate with each other. "None of the planes have properties or capabilities of being flown; the geometries are unimaginably horrendous from the point of view of flying; and the principles of propulsion make them resist rather than assist flying."

The world revealed by the *VS* is nonetheless a fascinating one, listing clothing for pilots ("silk, cotton, moss, hair, mica, leather

… purified by twenty-five processes") and varying seasonal diets ("in the four months of winter and snow, goat's-milk, yava and black-gram among grains, and flesh of sparrows"). There are sections on aircraft manufacture, with discussions on furnaces and metals ("artificial, corrupted, mud-born, found in mines, aquatic, mineral-born, vegetation-born, evolved from vermin, flesh-born, grown from salts, hairborn, and resultant from eggs"), sources of power ("fire, earth, air, sun, moon, water and sky"), and the different kinds of *vimanas*.

The *VS* is particularly obsessed with military aircraft and aerial combat. One chapter is devoted to mirrors and lenses, which can be used to neutralize both adverse atmospheric conditions and "enemy planes." Vedic enemies are capable of shooting rays and missiles, "poison fumes" are routinely used, and fighter aircraft need to be equipped with "mine-finders." The *VS* combines these menacing, modern-sounding technologies with a more organic sensibility, so that it often seems to be advocating a sustainable, locally sourced, crafts-based military production, one that combines, in one example, crystals, tree bark, and "essence of squash gourd" to manufacture a "reflected solar ray attracting mirror." And while the main aircraft in the *VS* are military in nature, it also details the occasional passenger aircraft. These are equipped with special kitchens operating "sacred fires," where food for the passengers can be cooked, which certainly seems a step up from clicking "Hindu vegetarian" as one's dietary option on an airline's website.

In this combination of a Brahminical mania for caste and purity with a fascination for military modernity, one can sense something of Sastry's obsessions as he dictated the *VS* in the early decades of the twentieth century. In its own way, the *VS* is an imaginative response to what must have seemed to Sastry a bewildering modern world, a colonial era in which traditional societies, including powerful empires, were collapsing—India's Mughal Empire had succumbed half a century ago—even as the aviation technology pioneered by the modern, warring industrial nations of the West went from the first powered flight by the Wright brothers in 1903 to military applications in World War I. The traditions of mysticism and Sanskritized knowledge that Sastry must have identified with would have seemed particularly ossified under colonial rule, which encouraged the idea of Hinduism as a religion guided by a small priestly sect of Brahmins with specialized knowledge while also denying that knowledge any practical applications beyond the directing of rigid social and religious customs. Sastry responded by conjuring up a world where traditional learning and modern technology could be brought together, where past and future lived simultaneously. What he created, then, was a hybrid, part holy book and part technical manual, with a guru in a cave on one end of its originating spectrum and a mechanical draftsman who had studied at an engineering college on the other.

It is impossible to say how much of this was an aspect of Brahminical Hindu culture feeling shortchanged by a world progressing rapidly around it and how much an imaginative claim being made on the most visibly dynamic aspects of a machine age. It depends on what one sees when reading a fairly representative passage like this: "When enemy planes with men intent on intercepting and destroying your *vimana* attack you with all the means at their disposal, the *viroopya-darpana* will frighten them into retreat or render them unconscious and leave you free to destroy or rout them. The *darpana*, like a magician, will change the appearance of your *vimana* into such frightening shapes that the attacker will be dismayed or paralyzed."

Yet for all its psychedelic inventiveness, and for what genre writers today would call "world-building," Sastry's imagining remained obscure and unknown in colonial India. Even in postcolonial India, as Josyer guided the *VS* out into the world, it stayed on the sidelines, one more quasi-miracle in a land of many quasi-miracles. Josyer, whom Lyon described as believing that "the Indo-Aryan civilization out of which Hindu India grew was the greatest, most advanced, and most enlightened civilization the world has ever known," was still representative of only one strand of Indian thinking. It needed the current age of wealthy, aspiring India to bring the *VS* and its attendant claims about Hindu India to the center stage of the national consciousness.

The last two decades of booming wealth in India, accompanied by its rising status in the world, have coincided with a time of increasingly aggressive Hindu nationalism. The same upward mobility that has made some Indians wealthy and professionally successful has also made them bellicose and insecure. The reasons for this are not hard to understand. Away from the glitter of India's billionaires, the endless appetite of its upper class for conspicuous consumption, and the industry of its middle-class technology workers, India remains a place where the vast majority is impoverished, where a quarter century of high-profile growth hasn't changed its shabby infrastructure, its unending violence against women and minorities, or its lagging behind even poor neighbors like Bangladesh in areas such as life expectancy, immunization, infant mortality, and education for girls. Even India's success as an outsourcing hub and consumer market is built on efficiently mimicking Western business practices and technological advances rather than by coming up with anything original of its own. There may be celebrations among its elites at the appointment of an Indian-origin CEO at Microsoft or the acquisition of Jaguar by Tata Motors, but there is still no Indian Microsoft or Indian Jaguar.

From this anxiety of imitation, it is a short step to seeking authenticity in texts from the past, even if one of those texts is itself a modern imitation. The effect is further magnified by a narrowly instrumental education, the shrinking of public debate, the subservience of media to business interests, the proliferation of social media, and an influential but alienated diaspora, especially in the United States, that seeks to find a glorious Hindu past that can be seen to have exceeded the very West upon which India's recent success depends so heavily. When this past does not exist, it has to be created, often in less imaginative ways than the manner in which Sastry fashioned the *VS*.

It has meant, for instance, the destruction of books with perspectives on ancient India that the Hindu right finds unpalatable. In 2001, when the Delhi University historian D. N. Jha wrote, in *The Myth of the Holy Cow*, that the ancient Vedic people were eaters of beef, he and his publisher were threatened, subjected to demonstrations, ritual book burnings, calls for the book to be banned, and a court order preventing its distribution. Jha's work was based on extensive archaeological and textual evidence, and his argument itself is widely accepted by professional historians in India and abroad, but it went against the Hindu right's insistence that beef-eating was an evil brought into the subcontinent by Muslims (a process it is determined to reverse by force, as in a recent ban in the state of Maharashtra that makes possession of beef punishable by a five-year jail term). Similarly, when University of Chicago scholar Wendy Doniger published *The Hindus: An Alternative History* in 2009, the campaign against it ran all the way from the United States to India, where the book's publishers, Penguin India, after a four-year legal battle, agreed to an out-of-court settlement that involved withdrawing all copies of the book and pulping them. Among the arguments against the book in the lawsuit initiated by Dina Nath Batra, founder of a Hindu right-wing educational organization and author of textbooks depicting ancient glories, like television and cars, was that "your approach is that of a woman hungry of sex."

In the absence of scholarly works that examine India's complex history, the ancient past imagined by the *VS* has flourished in ways Josyer could never have dreamed of in the '70s. The internet has seen to it that there are Facebook groups and YouTube animations on the *VS*, while the text itself is widely available online. It has made it possible for the *VS* to be cited as a canonical text at the Indian Science Congress and has even led to the attendant claim that it was an Indian, harnessing Vedic knowledge, who conducted the first powered flight in modern times, well before the Wright brothers.

This is said to have been another Sanskrit scholar, a man called Shivkar Bapuji Talpade, who in 1895 flew an unmanned, heavier-than-air machine at Chowpatty Beach in Bombay. Talpade is supposed to have built the aircraft on the basis of Vedic texts, one of which may have been the *VS*, powering his machine with mercury and solar energy and getting it to rise to 1,500 feet before it crashed. No one knows what this unmanned plane looked like, although if one goes by the illustrations in the *VS*, it could have resembled anything from a mechanical sparrow to an upside-down flowerpot with small propellers. If the flight happened, few details are available. No month or date for the flight is mentioned, just the year. The maharaja of Baroda, interested in technical innovations, is said to have been present at the flight, but scholars say there is no record of this in his papers. There are no contemporaneous accounts of the flight.

Among the believers of the Hindu right, this absence of evidence is attributed to British control over the media, which seemingly edited Talpade's invention out of history. But reports of the flight that do exist began proliferating just over a century later, in the 2000s, at the beginning of the fertile, ongoing period of the expansion of the economy and the reinvention of the Indian past. A story in the Indian newspaper *Business Standard*, discussing the references to Talpade that cropped up in the wake of the paper presented this January at the Indian Science Congress, states: "A quick search online shows that the event is most often discussed in forums on nationalism and pride [and] routinely outweighs research in these posts. One Hindi news channel even ran a segment recently declaring, '*Wright brothers wrong thhe*' (the Wright brothers were wrong)."

Zee News, the Hindi channel referred to here, did more than that. Intercutting illustrations from the *VS* and a portrait of Talpade with photographs of the Wright brothers and their biplane, it claimed that Talpade's machine was not just the modern world's first airplane but, since it had been operated with a remote control, could also rightfully be described as the world's first drone. It claimed that Talpade's design was eventually stolen from him by a British company under the false pretense of helping him and that it was quite likely this design that ended up in the hands of the Wright brothers.

The Bollywood film *Hawaizaada*, released a few weeks after Bodas's paper was presented at the Indian Science Congress, is somewhat more modest in its claims. It does not say that the Wright brothers filched Talpade's design. The film's trailer merely shows the words, "December 17, 1903: Wright Brothers Flew World's First Airplane in America," before displaying, "Eight Years Earlier, This Had Already Been Done by an Indian," just as it states, at the end of the film, "Three years back NASA commissioned a program to develop a mercury engine similar to what Shivkar Talpade had made 125 years ago." The British are still the villains in the film, determined to steal the *VS* from a mystical Sastry, who works on building his craft on a ship with the help of a rakish young Talpade. When Sastry dies, Talpade, in love with a dancer, completes the task, flying into the clouds with his beloved on his reconstructed Vedic *vimana*, even as the colonial policemen come huffing and puffing down to Chowpatty Beach.

Would Sastry have liked this Bollywood version of his life, or does this reinvention of a reinvention say more about contemporary India than the colonized India of his time? After all, even in the heyday of twentieth-century colonialism, Indian perspectives on military might and aircraft could accommodate perspectives other than that of mere emulation. Rabindranath Tagore, a contemporary of Sastry's, was an anti-colonialist as well as a critic of Indian nationalism, and he responded to the questions raised by powered flight quite differently. Flying for the first time in his life in 1932 from Calcutta to Iran, he recalled the mythical account in the *Mahabharata* of Arjuna being taken up into the air. Tagore, however, saw in this not power but a loss of intimacy with the earth, Arjuna's physical distancing leading to a moral distancing that allowed him to kill from the air without compunction. When Tagore arrived in Baghdad and was told by the air force chaplain there that British aircraft had been bombing Iraqi villages, he found his initial suspicions confirmed, reflecting—in terms that will be familiar to contemporary debates about drones—that "killing them from aircrafts is so easy, with so little fear of being killed in return, that the reality of killing becomes faint."

But Tagore's pacifism and humanism is not what the modern Hindu right seeks as it celebrates the ancient-modern wisdom of the *VS*. It has chosen, instead, to claim everything as its own, the first aircraft and the first drone, without much thought to what it might mean to possess such technology. In saying that the *VS* is an authentic text from the ancient past, it has created the past in the way it would have liked it to be, filled with Vedic heroes flying the skies in their *vimanas* and maintaining their caste laws. In this paradise of the past, there are no Buddhists or Muslims or Christians or Jews or left-wingers or women. The world that Sastry built is hermetically sealed from the world itself.

Yet the claim about the *VS* and its insertion into the national self-image is also a claim about the present. It says that Hindu India should rightfully be first among nations and cultures even by the measures of modernity, which are also the measures of the West. It is to say that India should be a place filled with heroes, sages, and inventors of fearsome devices rather than a supply source for technology workers with Western nicknames who put in endlessly long hours for global corporations, their upward mobility dependent on their willingness to be exploited by a West that has been ahead in this race since the time of Sastry. But if India is not what it should rightfully be, the *VS* and its supporting stories make it possible to believe that the enemies of Hindu India—centuries of Muslim rule, Western colonialism, secular modern elites—have stood between the glory of the past and what should be the glory of the present.

This view of India and its place in the world is a powerful and appealing one, but in the end it is to live in a kind of cage. In order to get out, one has to be able to make distinctions. There is no doubt that the modern technology that Sastry saw around him stemmed from brute exploitation and colonial domination, just as it is indisputable that even in later decades, after decolonization, India's contributions to knowledge were easily dismissed, forgotten, and appropriated by the West. Yet these grievances cannot be taken in isolation, since the same has happened and is happening to many other cultures and societies. And as far as India goes, the Hindu right, rather than functioning as a brave resistance, has been a willing collaborator in this process, attacking historians, banning books, and destroying ancient manuscripts (as happened when the Bhandarkar Oriental Research Institute was ransacked in 2004), disemboweling the past of all its complexity. In the place of that richness, it has been working hard to create myths it can be proud of, even if that means an ancient book created in modern times, filled with Vedic aircraft that cannot fly.

PART III

Chapter 7
Killing Gauri Lankesh

Political Assassinations and
the Silencing of Dissident Voices

Last September, as the journalist Gauri Lankesh was returning home from work, a man approached her in the driveway, his face obscured by a motorcycle helmet.* He fired a pistol as she ran toward her house, about ten feet away. She collapsed before she made it inside. Autopsy reports suggested she had been shot twice in the chest and once in the back. A fourth shot had missed or misfired. The footage from security cameras showed only two men on a motorcycle, including the helmeted shooter, a man about five feet tall, but the police suggested that two other men had also been involved, following the first pair on a second motorcycle.

The editor and publisher of a Bangalore weekly, the *Gauri Lankesh Patrike*, Lankesh was an outspoken left-wing journalist working in an India that, since the 2014 election of BJP leader Narendra Modi as prime minister, has become one of the world's most dangerous countries to be a reporter. But the BJP is only the most overt face of a Hindu right that comprises more than thirty loosely affiliated organizations. Together, they all subscribe to the

---

* First published in *Columbia Journalism Review*, Winter 2018.

virulent brand of Hindu nationalism known as Hindutva, and they have in recent years been associated with activities ranging from lynchings, riots, and bomb blasts to threats of rape, dismemberment, incarceration, and hanging of people critical of them and their sectarian idea of India.

In the 2017 Press Freedom Index compiled by Reporters Without Borders, India ranked 136 out of 180, a position quite out of keeping with India's image as the world's most populous democracy. Zimbabwe, before the fall of Robert Mugabe, came in at 127, while Afghanistan, mired in a grinding war, ranked 120th. Since 1992, according to the Committee to Protect Journalists, forty-three journalists have been killed in India. The number tallied by the International Federation of Journalists is far higher: seventy-three journalists killed since 2005. Nine journalists were killed in 2015, one of them allegedly set on fire by policemen working for a politician accused of rape. Five were murdered in 2016. In the cases of thirty journalists murdered since 2010 being tracked by the Indian media watchdog the Hoot, there has been exactly one conviction.

But who *was* Gauri Lankesh? Her assassination made her briefly, startlingly, visible everywhere, a slender figure with short, cropped hair, sometimes looking animated and sometimes appearing deeply introspective. Protests and vigils broke out throughout India, under posters and giant, colorful puppets proclaiming, "I am Gauri." Within a month of her death, her work had been posthumously granted the Anna Politkovskaya Award, named in honor of a Russian journalist who was assassinated in Moscow in 2006. By December, Navayana, a progressive publishing house in Delhi, had brought out a collection of Lankesh's writings and a Bangalore-based singer, Aarti Rao, released "Song for Gauri."

One understands why people might have responded in this way: Lankesh's life lends itself easily to the dramatic, to a biopic or a novel, a narrative illustrating through a single, individual portrait the tectonic shifts of a vast, populous country. Her struggle as a journalist and a woman was, after all, part of a larger struggle against Hindutva, just as her assassination was part of a larger web of assassinations of critics of Hindutva.

Yet the fact remains that while Lankesh's work was known to, and admired by, those connected to progressive politics and causes in India—people critical of Hindu nationalism, crony capitalism, sexism, and casteism—it was largely invisible beyond those realms. This was particularly true in the domain of national television and print media, outlets that seesaw between tawdry consumerism and rancorous nationalism, between retreating into strategic silence on controversial matters of the day and actively cheering on the right-wing politics of the BJP and its various vigilante armies.

Lankesh, who grew up in Bangalore, worked in the mid-'80s for the *Times of India*, the nation's largest daily newspaper. Having moved to Delhi with the *TOI*, she returned to Bangalore in 1989 and began reporting for *Sunday*, a now-defunct English-language magazine. Then, in the late nineties, she switched to Kannada-language television. This was a move laden with meaning. Not only was she uncomfortable with the language, her friends and associates say, but she was also stepping into the territory dominated by her father P. Lankesh. A well-known figure in the world of Kannada letters, P. Lankesh was a polymath, a literature professor, poet, playwright, filmmaker, and publisher of a weekly tabloid called *Lankesh Patrike*. The *Lankesh Patrike* did not accept advertisements, and it expressed what the Kannada-speaking journalist Krishna Prasad, former editor of the newsmagazine *Outlook* and writer of the incisive media and politics blog *Churumuri*, described to me as an "eclectic world view," erudite and literary while also being political and punchy.

When Lankesh's father died in 2000, she and her brother, Indrajit, assumed charge of the weekly. Their third sibling, Kavitha, a filmmaker, did not take on a role at the paper. While Indrajit became the publisher at *Lankesh Patrike*, Lankesh was responsible for editorial. This, Prasad notes, was a significant transition for her. Not only did she now have to write in Kannada while also running the weekly, but she also had to manage a shift in focus from the urban, fluffy issues dominating corporate English media to rural issues that involved a more critical, engaged kind of journalism and that was central to the mission of *Lankesh Patrike*. In an interview Lankesh gave shortly after she took over, she said she had deliberately distanced herself from the weekly while her father was running it "because it is such a strident, hard-hitting paper, and I was working for the mainstream English media." She added that she had been stagnating in English-language journalism, while her slightly cryptic references to "being alone" and "personal confusions" also hinted at the difficulty of being a single, independent-minded woman—her marriage to the journalist Chidanand Rajghatta had ended in divorce in the early nineties—in a patriarchal, conservative milieu.

§

While some skeptics questioned at the time whether Lankesh, given her lack of editing experience and previous involvement with the paper, could fill her father's role, she embraced the transformation. She took an increasingly critical position on what Prasad calls "the upsurge of Hindutva forces of polarization" around the country and in particular in Karnataka. In 2002, she protested the Hindu right's attempt to claim that the eleventh-century Sufi shrine of Baba Budan Giri, 170 miles west of Bangalore, where both Hindus and Muslims had worshipped for centuries, belonged exclusively to Hindus. "She courted arrest on the streets during the protest," says her former husband Rajghatta, who remained friends with her after their divorce and is now a Washington-based columnist for the *Times of India*. "She was taking an increasingly leftist stand, always siding with the underdog."

As Lankesh became more involved in political questions, she traveled in June 2004 to the southwestern region of Malnad to attend a press conference held by members of the Indian ultra-left movement variously referred to as Naxalites or Maoists. One of the Naxalites she met there was Saketh Rajan, a former Bangalore classmate and the son of an army officer, a radical who had written histories of Karnataka and worked as an environmentally conscious, muckraking journalist before becoming a guerrilla. Eight months after the meeting, Rajan was dead, shot down in the kind of extrajudicial execution referred to by the police in India as an "encounter." Lankesh wrote an article about the killing. Her brother Indrajit, an occasional filmmaker and television personality who last year officially joined the BJP, citing Modi as the inspiration behind his decision, refused to publish the article, apparently because it was much too sympathetic to the Naxalites. Lankesh claimed he threatened her with a revolver.

Following the dispute, Lankesh left her father's former paper and decided to start her own, the *Gauri Lankesh Patrike*. The seemingly minor adjustment in title had a wider significance. It brought into even sharper focus her status as a woman who had positioned herself against the dominant currents in India. Instead of denigrating the Naxalites, she was attempting to get the government into dialogue with them. An op-ed she wrote for her paper in 2003, translated and republished by the *New York Times* in the weeks following her death, talked about the commonality and mutual curiosity of Indians and Pakistanis staring at each other across the heavily militarized border between the two nations.

Younger activists who often split along lines of identity and ideology spoke of Lankesh's successful attempts to mediate between them—leftists, Muslims, Dalits, women, the indigenous—on the basis of their common antipathy to Hindutva and its dystopian blueprint for the future. Rana Ayyub*, an independent journalist whose book, *Gujarat Files*, is an account of her undercover investigation of bureaucrats and police officials involved in the anti-Muslim pogroms of 2002, recalled in an email her friendship with Lankesh, "She published my book *Gujarat Files* in Kannada despite the threats and intimidation she was subjected to."

§

Although the southern state of Karnataka, of which Bangalore is the capital, is currently run by the centrist Congress Party, it remains a hotbed of activity of the Hindu right. This often manifests itself in violent forms. Two years before Lankesh's murder, the scholar M. M. Kalburgi was gunned down in his living room in Dharwad, a small city 260 miles northwest of Bangalore. Before that, in the neighboring state of Maharashtra, Govind Pansare, an author and left-wing trade unionist, and Narendra Dabholkar, a doctor and an activist, were murdered.

Like Lankesh, all three were critics of Hindutva and wrote in local languages (Lankesh and Kalburgi in Kannada; Pansare and Dabholkar in Marathi). All were killed in a similar manner, shot by motorcycle-borne, helmeted men who had used a 7.65-millimeter pistol of the kind referred to in India as "improvised" in recognition of their local, illegal manufacturing origins.

---

* Ayyub, who is now a columnist for the *Washington Post*, has herself been extensively targeted by the Modi government and its army of right-wing trolls, from a doctored clip of her purportedly performing sexual acts circulated on social media, to having her bank accounts frozen.

Nevertheless, there were some efforts at the beginning to suggest that Lankesh's violent death was sui generis, with the police claiming the men they suspected of the crime were contract killers. The Congress chief minister of Karnataka, K. Siddaramaiah, also initially suggested that Lankesh's death was the work of "organized crime," but added his government was "confident of nabbing the culprits and bringing them to book at the earliest." Months later, the culprits have not been nabbed and brought to book. At the same time, the stalled state of investigations into the murders of Kalburgi, Pansare, and Dabholkar—the latter was assassinated in August 2013, more than four years ago—as well as the ongoing intimidation in India of the media, public intellectuals, activists, and ordinary citizens, raises the question of whether justice will be carried out any time soon, or at all.

In recent years, Lankesh's opposition to right-wing Hinduism had taken the form of claiming that the Lingayats, the community in Karnataka to which she belonged, should be given the status of a separate religion, an argument that would have angered the powerful, conservative faction of the Lingayats, the Veerashaivas, who saw themselves and, by extension, all Lingayats as part of the Hindu fold. Kalburgi, the scholar assassinated in August 2015, had also been a Lingayat. Using the twelfth-century texts central to the Lingayat movement, Kalburgi too had made a similar argument about Lingayats being quite distinct from caste-based Hinduism. After receiving threats, he had been provided with police protection. Fifteen days after he asked his bodyguards to be withdrawn, he was killed.

"Lingayats have been recruited as the BJP's largest voting bloc," Raghu Karnad, an editor at the nonprofit news site the Wire who was friendly with Lankesh, told me in an email, making the issue especially controversial in the run-up to Karnataka's state assembly elections in May. Karnad, who first met Lankesh in person at a vigil for Kalburgi, thinks it was this nexus of local and national politics that led to Lankesh's death. "A declaration that Lingayats are a minority religion is the single worst thing that could happen to the BJP, when it was planning to eliminate the Congress in Karnataka."

Yet whatever specific combination of local and national interests was involved, the broad finger of suspicion points, inexorably, to members of the Hindu right, determined to eliminate its ideological enemies. Pansare and Dabholkar, who had been assassinated in the neighboring state of Maharashtra, were not involved specifically in the Lingayat question. They were part of what is referred to as the rationalist tradition of southern and western India, strongly committed to a scientific temperament, debunking superstition and the power of godmen and gurus, and opposed to both the political violence of Hindu majoritarianism as well as its social practice of enforcing caste and gender hierarchies. Pansare had promoted intercaste marriages. Dabholkar had been attempting to get the state government to introduce a law banning superstitious practices. His death finally provoked the government into action, and in December 2013, it passed the astonishing-sounding "Maharashtra Prevention and Eradication of Human Sacrifice and Other Inhuman, Evil and Aghori Practices and Black Magic Act."

Yet the investigation of the killings of Dabholkar, Pansare, and Kalburgi remained tardy, often at cross purposes. The inquiry into Dabholkar's killing, the oldest of the four cases, was botched by the Maharashtra Police and transferred, through the orders of the Bombay High Court, to the Central Bureau of Investigation (CBI), a federal agency. The Maharashtra Police continues, however, to investigate the Pansare killing, while the Karnataka Police handles the Kalburgi and Lankesh killings. The National Investigation Agency (NIA), a federal counter-terrorism body, is also involved. The involvement of different police agencies, with coordination required across bureaucratic boundaries, may be one of the factors responsible for the slow pace of the investigations. Abhay Nevagi, who has been representing the Dabholkar, Pansare, and Kalburgi families pro bono in a public interest litigation urging the Bombay High Court to demand accountability from the investigating bodies, says that there have been twenty-four court hearings to date.

And yet, in spite of the lack of coordination, the cross-communication between the investigating bodies, and perhaps their unwillingness to dig very deep or very far, certain patterns have emerged that connect all four killings. According to the ballistic report of the Karnataka Police, which looked at the bullets fired in the assassinations, two 7.65-millimeter pistols were used in the killing of Pansare in February 2015. One of those pistols matched with the single weapon used to kill Dabholkar in August 2013, while the other matched with the weapon used to kill Kalburgi in August 2015. "The CBI laboratory has confirmed these matches," Nevagi tells me. Now, reports from the forensic labs in Bangalore appear to have confirmed that the weapon used to kill Pansare and Kalburgi was also the weapon used to murder Lankesh. A Bangalore-based reporter who did not wish to be identified told me his own sources in the Karnataka Police had confirmed this match as well.

The suspects around these linked pistols are members of a shadowy Hindu organization called the Sanatan Sanstha (SS), with headquarters in Goa, a state bordering Maharashtra and Karnataka. Two members of the SS, Vinay Pawar and Sarang Akolkar, are suspected of being the gunmen in the Pansare and Dabholkar cases. They are also wanted in connection with a bomb blast in a Goa marketplace in 2009 where two other members of the SS died—this explains the involvement of the counter-terrorism NIA—but the government has so far been unable to trace them. Two other SS members were also arrested for involvement in the Dabholkar and Pansare murders, a doctor called Virendra Tawade and a man called Samir Gaikwad, with the latter currently out on bail.

The SS has responded to the charges by parading thirty-one lawyers at a court hearing and threatening on social media to sue media organizations. One of its websites claims it "exposed corrupt practices of Comrade Pansare and Dr Dabholkar." Dabholkar's son, Hamid, however, noted in his affidavit to the Bombay High Court that his father's photograph had been displayed on the SS website before the murder with a "red cross across his face."

§

Lankesh was the third journalist killed in India in 2017, but not the last. Even as I spoke on the phone to Prasad about her death, he was on his way to Agartala, capital of the northeastern state of Tripura, to cover the murder of a cable television reporter who had been killed during a political demonstration. Tripura, like Karnataka, holds assembly elections this year, and the BJP is a prime contender there as well.

In other states on the frontline of armed conflicts between the government and the local population, such as Kashmir and Chattisgarh, it is dangerous to be a journalist even when there are no elections on the horizon. Under the pretenses of protecting national security, soldiers and police personnel (not to mention gangsters and vigilantes) intimidate media critical of government policies with complete impunity. In Kashmir, the government regularly shuts down social media, television channels, and newspapers. Of the forty-five attacks on journalists in India recorded in 2017 by the Hoot, six were in Kashmir. In Chattisgarh, where mining companies, encouraged by the state and paramilitary forces, are facing off against indigenous populations and Naxalite guerrilla forces, journalists face dangers ranging from being denied hotel rooms and their phones being tapped to threats and arbitrary arrests by the police.

Journalists, however, are not the only ones under threat, as the killings of Kalburgi and the rationalists make clear. Sometimes, it appears as if the enemy is information itself, along with transparency, exposure, critical thinking—anything and everything that might be seen as characteristic of a free, open society. In the central Indian state of Madhya Pradesh, in a scandal involving admission to medical colleges that implicated the top BJP officials in the state, including the chief minister Shivraj Singh Chouhan, more than forty whistleblowers, accused, and witnesses—doctors, medical students, policemen, and civil servants—turned up mysteriously dead over a period of three years. Ironically, national media took notice of the case, known as the Vyapam scam, only in 2015 when Akshay Singh, a television reporter investigating the death of a nineteen-year-old medical student—a death that had been passed off by the police as a suicide in spite of the strangulation marks on her body—himself collapsed and died in the middle of an interview with the student's family.

The Vyapam deaths, at least, sparked a brief phase of outrage within India's mainstream media. But this was an exception. More recently, the national media has largely refused to touch two recent stories involving Amit Shah, president of the BJP and Modi's consigliere. In October, the Wire reported that a company owned by Shah's son, Jay Shah, had increased its revenues from approximately $780 in 2014–15 to $12.5 million the year following Modi's election. A year later, the company ceased business altogether. The Wire's scoop received scant attention from other English and Hindi outlets.

The same was true of an article in the Delhi-based magazine *Caravan* in November 2017 about the suspicious circumstances surrounding the death of Brijgopal Harkishan Loya, a forty-eight-year-old judge. Apparently a healthy man, Loya was said to have died suddenly of a heart attack on December 1, just weeks before he was scheduled to try Shah in a case about an extrajudicial execution that had taken place in Gujarat under his watch as home minister. An unknown functionary of the Rashtriya Swayamsevak Sangh (RSS), the mass organization that serves as the fountainhead of the Hindu right, helpfully turned up out of nowhere to contact Loya's family and explain that the body was being sent to them for funeral rites. Less than a month later, Shah was acquitted by the judge who took over the case from Loya.

The caution of the national media can in part be explained by pressure and intimidation. The Wire was served with a criminal defamation suit by lawyers for Jay Shah, with the court issuing a gag order in the case until the trial is complete. A CBI raid was ordered last June on the residence of the owners of NDTV, a television channel perceived as being critical of the BJP. The same channel was forced off the air for twenty-four hours in November 2016 as punishment for allegedly revealing strategic details about an anti-terror operation. Yet external pressure is only a partial explanation for the complacence of the national media, which from the owners down to editorial staff often seems to be a willing participant in the project of Hindu nationalism.

Many of the journalists I interviewed for this story had been forced out from earlier positions when articles they wrote or published ran afoul of the Hindu right. Prasad stepped down from *Outlook* in 2016 because a report he had published had resulted in a defamation lawsuit filed by a BJP functionary. He left voluntarily, he tells me, out of respect for the owners who had come under immense pressure. The story, a five-part investigation painstakingly reported over three months by independent journalist Neha Dixit, detailed the trafficking of thirty-one indigenous girls, ages three to eleven, by the RSS, ostensibly for the purpose of Hinduizing them. Hartosh Singh Bal, the political editor of *Caravan* who published the Loya story after it was brought to him by a journalist who had it turned down at the magazine he was working for, was himself fired from his previous job at *Open* magazine just before the 2014 election that brought Modi and the BJP to power. He was seen as being too critical of the BJP, he told me, and has since taken his previous employers to court for being dismissed without being given a reason.

§

Lankesh's work and life take on even greater significance against this wider context. By most accounts, she and her tabloid were struggling by the time of her death. Its circulation was low, somewhere between 10,000 and 15,000. She published textbooks and nonfiction to finance her paper, and her own English writing subsidized her Kannada journalism. But in November 2016, her column for *Bangalore Mirror* was canceled, reducing her income even further.

Friends and associates of Lankesh mention her calls, often connected to efforts to raise money for the paper. She had stopped paying her insurance premiums, Karnad wrote in a tribute published by *n+1* shortly after her death. The house she lived in, Lankesh's sister Kavitha tells me, had been a gift to her from their mother. Prasad, who blogged about Lankesh in the immediate aftermath of her killing, wrote that Lankesh had called him in April and said that she had only enough money left to cover a month's expenses. The sudden cancellation of large-denomination banknotes by the Modi government in November 2016 had devastated newsstand sales, which her publication depended on. "When her end came, the ignition was on in Toyota's cheapest offering in India," Prasad wrote.

If there was this, a steady erosion of the material conditions of her journalism, there were also the shock waves consisting of lawsuits, threats, and character assassination. In 2016, Lankesh was found guilty by a lower court in a defamation case filed by two BJP politicians who had been accused, in an article published in 2008, of defrauding a jeweler. "Hope other journos take note," the head of the BJP's information and technology department tweeted after the verdict. Lankesh felt she was being targeted for her politics and intended to challenge the verdict.

The virulence did not ease up after her death. Because she was buried rather than cremated, in keeping with Lingayat practices, there were attempts to argue that she was Christian, as if this justified her killing. A man from Gujarat describing himself as a "garment manufacturer" and "Hindu Nationalist," one of 1,779 accounts followed at the time by Modi, tweeted, "One bitch dies a dog's death all the puppies cry in the same tune." Another man posted on Facebook, "Not an iota of sympathy for Lankesh, and the killers should have shredded her body with bullets and even blasted apart her apartment." He also issued a hit list demanding that five women, all publicly visible authors, journalists, and commentators with politics ranging from liberal to left-wing, also be killed.

There is no reason to believe these comments, and the people who make them, are anomalies. The Hindu right, in the run-up to the 2014 elections, popularized the term "presstitute," a word that captures perfectly its loathing of a free press as well as of the underclass, marginalized women who make a living as sex workers. It remains a depressingly popular hashtag on Indian social media, accompanied by demented rants and fake news attempting to incite violence against its enemies.

§

The final issue of *Gauri Lankesh Patrike* had, in fact, been called "In the Age of False News," with an editorial by Lankesh that called out the Hindu right and its "lie factories." She had noted the proliferation of rumors and right-wing abuse, and the deliberate stoking of violence, including by troll farms that target women, religious minorities, and people of opposing ideologies. There is no doubt the Hindu right is at the forefront of this.

Yet the possibility that the SS, a relatively recent entrant into the fold of right-wing Hinduism, might have been behind the murders of Lankesh and the others raises an even more disturbing possibility. It suggests that under the tutelage of the BJP, a model of entrepreneurial Hindutva has been unleashed, with new organizations that carry out independent acts of violence, though with the tacit support and encouragement of establishment Hindutva. Dhirendra Jha, a political journalist with the news site Scroll and author of the book *Shadow Armies: Fringe Organizations and Foot Soldiers of Hindutva*, notes that Hindu right groups like the SS are connected to their parent organization and yet are not "direct projections."

The SS, set up as a charitable trust in 1991, was founded by Jayant Balaji Athavale. Beginning as a hypnotherapist in Britain in the '70s, Athavale transformed himself first into the founding guru of the SS before achieving, in 2015, an even more remarkable transformation: he became, Jha's book notes, a living god as manifested by his "hair turning golden; divine particles falling from his body; the symbol of OM appearing on his fingernails, forehead and tongue; and various fragrances from his body." The seizure of psychotropic drugs from an SS ashram complex in Maharashtra in September 2016—in quantities, Dabholkar's son, a psychiatrist, noted in his affidavit to the Bombay High Court, "only required by a mental hospital"—adds to the perception that the group has many of the characteristics of a cult.

The larger ambition of the SS, however, is the establishment of a Hindu *rashtra*, or nation, by 2023, which suggests the point where cult and Hindutva converge, and where the shadow world of assassinations meets the realm of electoral politics. "The choice of the date," Jha says, "seems to be connected to the assumption that Modi will win the election in 2019 and give them another five years to achieve their target, around 2023 or 2024."

§

According to those close to the investigation into Lankesh's killing, there are signs the police may be close to solving the crime.* "They are looking at a little more evidence," Lankesh's sister Kavitha tells me. If so, it will be a welcome change from the stasis that seems to have infected the investigations into other slain critics of Hindutva. But will solving the Lankesh case offer answers or will it open up further questions?

Because whoever the killers turn out to be, Lankesh's death has to be attributed to more than the men who pulled the trigger and rode the motorcycles, or even those shadowy figures who planned the assassination. She was killed by the culture of

---

* By August 2023, the police had arrested 18 out of its 19 suspects, including the shooter. However, the police have been unable to prove that the accused were active members of the SS at the time of the killing, even though they had all been connected to SS in the past and were in possession of an SS "killing manual" that valorized the assassination of Hindus who were critical of the faith. The murder weapon, also used in the killings of Pansare and Kalburgi, was apparently thrown into a river and has not been recovered. Sixty witnesses have been cross-examined so far, but there are many more left to be questioned and the trial is expected to go on for another two to three years.

impunity promoted by India's Hindu right, which goes all the way up to political leaders of the Hindu right, including Modi. This culture flourishes because of the compliant media that supports it and the talking heads who rationalize it. Most distressingly, it is nourished by a broad swath of Hindu society—mostly well-to-do, urban, professional, upper-caste—that either chooses to ignore the violence or actively cheers it on. There is no police force in the world that can address such widespread social and political malaise. Perhaps, all that is available is the solidarity that Lankesh herself practiced, the forging of connections between people and the importance given to politics, ideas, and words. Kavitha tells me she asked her sister to act a small part in *Summer Holidays*, a Kannada children's film she directed and that will be released this summer. "She played an activist," Kavitha says, laughing. "She was very good at it."

Chapter 8
Manufacturing Evidence

The Bhima Koregaon Conspiracy
and the Plot to Imprison India's Activists

In April 2018, a large group of policemen arrived at the Delhi flat of Rona Wilson, a forty-seven-year-old human rights activist.* They had traveled from Pune in the western state of Maharashtra, and appeared, accompanied by Delhi police officials, at Wilson's single-room flat at 6 a.m. For the next eight hours, they scoured the modest premises, searching the files on Wilson's laptop and rifling through his books. Annoyed and short of sleep, he asked that they be put back in place after they had been scrutinized. When the police eventually left, they took away Wilson's Hewlett-Packard laptop, a SanDisk thumb drive, and his mobile phone.

Seven weeks later, the police were back at Wilson's flat, this time to arrest him. He was accused of conspiring to assassinate the prime minister, Narendra Modi, and planning to overthrow the ruling BJP government. Evidence of these crimes had allegedly been found on his laptop. Wilson was flown to Pune, charged under India's anti-terror law, and incarcerated. More than three years after the arrest, he remains in prison.

---

* First published in the *Guardian*, August 12, 2021.

Wilson, who appeared in press photographs with flowing, shoulder-length hair, squeezed between two plainclothes policemen in the backseat of an unmarked van, seems an unlikely candidate for violent conspiracy. A Malayalam-speaking Christian who grew up in the southern state of Kerala, Wilson's life in Delhi had been wholly devoted to campaigning on behalf of political prisoners. He made visits to inmates in Tihar Jail, India's largest prison, to lawyers' offices to help with campaigns for their release, and to dozens of media organizations in the center of New Delhi to raise awareness of the plight of those he believed had been falsely incarcerated.

Just before his arrest, Wilson had applied to the PhD program in political science at Surrey University, and was hoping to leave for the UK if he managed to get a scholarship. The documentary filmmaker Sanjay Kak, who has known Wilson for nearly two decades and worked with him on campaigns for the release of political prisoners, described him as completely devoted to the cause. "Rona in many ways exemplifies an Indian kind of activist—quiet, self-effacing and yet deeply committed to what they do," he said. "The tragedy of what has happened to him is that he has been drawn in by the very machine he worked so hard to dismantle all his life."

Wilson is one of sixteen people arrested since June 2018 for their part in an alleged Maoist conspiracy to foment an uprising against Modi's government. The origin of this so-called conspiracy was traced to a festival called the Elgaar Parishad (meaning "loud assembly") held in Pune on December 31, 2017. Organized by two progressive retired judges, the festival was looking ahead to the 200th anniversary of a famous Dalit victory in the nearby village of Bhima Koregaon in 1818, when historically oppressed Dalit soldiers serving in a British regiment defeated an upper-caste Hindu army.

During the festival, speakers criticized the ruling BJP and the Rashtriya Swayamsevak Sangh (RSS), often described as its paramilitary branch, for their promotion of a Hindu majoritarian state and for their attempts to subvert India's constitution, which upholds the principles of religious and ethnic equality. The next day, January 1, 2018, clashes broke out as Dalits converging upon Bhima Koregaon were beaten and pelted with stones by mobs waving the distinctive saffron flags of the Hindu right. One man was killed in the riots, and property was smashed and burned.

Although those initially accused of instigating the violence were two local men with long-standing links to the Hindu right, the investigation quickly altered course. By April, the focus of police inquiries had become a convoluted plot involving "urban Naxals"—a catchphrase popularized by the Hindu right for activists and intellectuals with progressive leanings—operating as a front for underground Maoist groups and inciting Dalits to rise up against the government. This alleged incitement to insurrection was named the "Bhima Koregaon conspiracy."

There are thousands of political detainees currently held in India's prisons, but more than any other mass arrest, the Bhima Koregaon case shows the way Modi's government cracks down on criticism of its Hindu nationalist ideology and disguises its harsh repression as part of a war on terror.

Wilson had been nowhere near the Elgaar Parishad event. In fact, he was not even in Maharashtra at the time. According to his legal team, he was in Delhi. After the raid on his flat, the police, however, claimed that an analysis of Wilson's computer and thumb drive had revealed several incriminating documents, including a letter in which Wilson had written about "targeting" Modi's "road-shows" in "another Rajiv Gandhi type incident"—a reference to the assassination of India's former prime minister by a Tamil Tiger suicide bomber in 1991.

On June 6, 2018, the day the police arrested Wilson in Delhi, they also took in four other activists in different parts of India who had allegedly worked with Wilson on the conspiracy. Like Wilson, the other detainees—Surendra Gadling (age fifty-three), a Dalit lawyer; Sudhir Dhawale (fifty-two), a Dalit writer; Shoma Sen (sixty-three), a feminist literature professor, and Mahesh Raut (thirty-four), a land rights activist—had no record of violence.

Their activism, often challenging the excesses of the state and Hindu-right organizations, was a matter of public record, carried out largely in courts, panels, rallies, and press conferences. The government nevertheless extended its net further over the following two years, arresting people in Hyderabad, Delhi, and Ranchi, until by October 2020 the total number of those detained had risen to sixteen.

Known to activists and the media as the BK16, the detainees included Anand Teltumbde (seventy-one), a Dalit public intellectual who is married to the granddaughter of B. R. Ambedkar, the Dalit architect of the Indian constitution; Sudha Bhardwaj (fifty-nine), a Boston-born lawyer who represents workers and indigenous people in central India; and Stan Swamy, an octogenarian activist and Jesuit priest suffering from Parkinson's. Swamy, arrested last October, was denied bail by a judge who refused to accept that his health was precarious. He contracted COVID-19 while in prison and died on July 5 this year, which prompted widespread global condemnation but drew no response from Modi.

Wilson remains in Taloja men's prison in Mumbai, as do most of his fellow accused. Fourteen of the BK16 have been denied bail. The only exceptions are the eighty-one-year-old poet and activist Varavara Rao, who tested positive for COVID-19 last year, and who will return to prison when his six-month bail comes to an end this month; and Gadling, who has been given one week's bail, starting next week, to perform rites for his mother on the first anniversary of her death.

Mihir Desai, a lawyer representing the BK16, described their long incarceration without trial as characteristic of India's draconian anti-terror law, the Unlawful Activities Prevention Act (UAPA), which makes getting bail almost impossible. Once the trial begins, it could take anywhere from five to ten years. "Most of them have been in jail for three years already, and the trial is a long way away," Desai said with some weariness. "The prosecution claims that it has two hundred witnesses. Just imagine how long it will take to question them all."

§

The government's case against the BK16 is notable both for its sheer size—apart from 200 witnesses, the charges filed against the BK16 run to a total of 17,000 pages—as well as the seemingly outlandish nature of the plot it claims to have uncovered. In the electronic communications allegedly found by the investigation and leaked to a compliant mainstream media, Wilson and his co-accused freely address one another by their first names while discussing plans to acquire arms and ammunition for the assassination of the prime minister and to forming an "anti-fascist front" as a prelude to an uprising.

The charge sheets filed by the police and the federal anti-terror body, the National Investigation Agency (NIA), are filled with wild, unproven, and possibly unprovable, assertions. "In order to further activities of CPI (Maoist) on an international level," reads the charge against Teltumbde, "he used to attend international conferences under the guise of his academic visits at Canada, Pakistan, the USA, France etc. In the said conferences, he used to exchange literature on ideology, training and working strategy of CPI (Maoist) with international communist organizations." The charge sheets and evidence list include bewildering diagrams titled "Mobile Connectivity Chart" and "Email Connectivity Chart," a photocopy of *Marx for Beginners*, and a "book with cover picture of lady wearing white colour sari with written thereon in English words as 'Accused INDIAN ARMY.'"

Further evidence comes from an assortment of computers, mobile phones, cameras, SIM cards, and thumb drives seized from the accused. But the information discovered on these electronic devices is dubious, and not just because of the suspiciously bad writing and transparent scheming on display in the emails allegedly exchanged between Wilson and "Comrade Prakash" (supposedly the code name for an underground militant).

Alarmed by the suspect nature of the arrests and charges, activists and lawyers working to free the BK16 got in touch with the human rights section of the American Bar Association. The ABA looked into the judicial records in the case and, in a preliminary report in October 2019, found that they raised "serious concerns of procedural irregularities, abuse of process and violations of fundamental human rights." Through the ABA, Wilson's lawyers approached a US-based digital forensics firm, Arsenal Consulting, to dig further into the case.

In July 2020, a hard drive from Mumbai containing cloned copies of Wilson's laptop and thumb drives arrived at Arsenal's office in Massachusetts. In February 2021, Arsenal presented its initial findings in the first of a series of reports on the BK16. "We had sent it to them thinking that evidence might have been planted on the devices by the police after the raid," a member of the defense said. But Arsenal's findings astonished them. They appeared to show that incriminating documents had been planted on computers belonging to the accused in a clandestine operation dating back years before the alleged role of the BK16 in the Bhima Koregaon riots.

Studying clones of the laptop and thumb drive seized by the police from Wilson, Arsenal came to the conclusion that hackers had planted malware on Wilson's laptop twenty-two months before the police showed up on his doorstep. Through a series of emails to Wilson purportedly from the account of Varavara Rao, the poet, the attacker got Wilson to open what he thought was a Dropbox link, but was actually a link to what the Arsenal report identified as a "malicious command and control server." Once the malware was installed, the hacker deposited thirty-two incriminating documents—including the letter discussing the assassination of Modi—on Wilson's laptop over a period of nearly a year. Throughout, according to Arsenal's analysts, the attacker was able to control Wilson's laptop, conceal the fact that incriminating documents had been planted, and spy on Wilson "browsing websites, submitting passwords, composing emails, and editing documents."

Before Arsenal's reports, other organizations had discovered that associates of the BK16 were being targeted. An investigation by Citizen Lab Canada found that between February and May 2019, the phones of Teltumbde, who had not been arrested at that point, as well as more than twenty people connected to the BK16, had been targeted by the military-grade Pegasus spyware sold to governments by the Israeli firm NSO. In September and October that year, a study by a digital division of Amnesty International showed that many of the same people were sent a series of emails containing malware.

In July 2021, the *Guardian* and a consortium of news organizations revealed that Pegasus spyware had been used by a number of repressive governments around the world to spy on human rights defenders, activists, and journalists. Modi's government was said to be among those using Pegasus, and it was reportedly found to be targeting opposition politicians, journalists, and activists in India. Among potential targets were, it was claimed, eight of the BK16, including Rona Wilson.

The NIA has dismissed Arsenal's findings, saying the company has "no *locus standi* to give opinion," and noting that the Indian government's own forensics lab discovered no malware on Wilson's devices. Mark Spencer, president of Arsenal, said in response: "Arsenal digital forensics reports are extremely detailed, thorough and clear—they speak for themselves." When the *Washington Post* contacted three different digital forensics experts in the US with Arsenal's first report, all three stated that Arsenal's findings were "sound." These findings were also supported by an investigation by the Delhi-based magazine *Caravan*, which had examined a copy of Wilson's hard drive in March 2020 and discovered malware pointing to "manipulation of evidence" in the case against the BK16.

Arsenal uses a forensic technique that can accurately identify the date documents were uploaded. They were convinced that the planting of malware and incriminating documents on Wilson's devices were not isolated events. They say that the attacker who had infected Wilson's devices with the incriminating documents had also been targeting Wilson's co-accused in the BK16 for more than four years.

An expert who chose to remain anonymous but who is extremely familiar with Arsenal's investigations—detailed across three reports, the latest of them released in July 2021—described the attacks as revealing "a massive infrastructure" involving "layers of bogus accounts used by the attackers, many different kinds of malware, different 'crypters,' compiling source code just prior to launching attacks, compromising email accounts to deploy malware in some situations, and using email forgery services."

Taken together, this suggests that behind the alleged Bhima Koregaon conspiracy there is another conspiracy—one that originates from entities whose interests coincide entirely with Modi and his Hindu-right government.

§

The cascade of events that started with a peaceful gathering and ended with the roundup of the BK16 under the anti-terror act reveals a chillingly familiar picture of repression throughout Modi's India, one that follows a well-established pattern of turning victims into perpetrators by manipulating the legal system.

In January 2020 a new law, the Citizenship Amendment Act (CAA), came into effect. It threatened to discriminate against Muslims and strip them of their rights as Indian nationals. Thousands of protesters took to the streets of Delhi—not just Muslims, but a cross section of people who had come together in solidarity. On February 23, a wave of violence broke out in the city when the protesters were attacked by thugs of the Hindu right and the Delhi Police. By the time the riots ended, fifty-three people had died in the clashes, two-thirds of whom were Muslim.

A report by *Caravan* in September 2020 detailed the state's shocking complicity in the violence. Like the Dalit commemoration in Bhima Koregaon two years before, the protests had started out as peaceful gatherings. Yet Hindu-right leaders portrayed the protesters as aggressive, ignorant Muslims opposing rights for Hindus, instigating violence that eventually turned into large-scale rioting.

After the violence came the conspiracy theories. On March 11, 2020, an organization calling itself the Group of Intellectuals and Academicians—a group with no known intellectual or academic credentials, but with close links to the Hindu right—submitted a report to the government suggesting that the violence in Delhi had been the work of that bogeyman of the right, the

Urban Naxal–Jihadi network. Soon a series of arrests began, focusing not on the widely documented perpetrators of the violence and those who had goaded them on, but on protesters.

As with the BK16, the instrument used to go after the protesters was the anti-terror law. Although the UAPA was first passed in 1967 and was updated in 2008 by the Congress government, Modi has seized upon it with vigor to pursue opponents of his Hindu nationalist movement. In the four years after Modi became prime minister, cases brought under the act almost doubled, to 5,102. In July 2019, shortly after Modi was reelected, the act was further revised to allow the government to designate any individual as a terrorist without having to establish their membership or association with any banned organizations.

On May 16, 2020, Asif Iqbal Tanha (twenty-five), a member of a group that had been at the forefront of protests against the CAA, was arrested at his flat in Jamia Nagar in southeast Delhi. After he was allowed out on bail, in June, I spoke to him in the apartment of a fellow activist. Sitting in a room with a table holding at least fifty bulky folders—copies of the anti-terror charges against protesters—Tanha described how he had been accused of buying a SIM card with the help of false documents and passing the card on to another protester.

"I've never been to the mobile phone shop they accused me of visiting, never met the man they said I bought the SIM card from, and never had a SIM card other than the one in my phone, which the police had seized more than a month before they decided to arrest me," Tanha told me. He said he had nevertheless been subjected to a bewildering sequence of charges, interrogations, arrests, and court appearances. Held overnight at the office of the Delhi Police special cell—an anti-terror division notorious for torture and extrajudicial executions—and then incarcerated in Tihar Jail, he had been beaten by special cell officers, he said.

"Seven or eight people punched and kicked me. Finally, I was left alone but with a bright halogen light on my eyes all night long. When I was moved to Tihar, I was again assaulted by officials as well as by prisoners who accused me of being a jihadi."

Civil rights campaigner Nadeem Khan described the crackdown on anti-CAA protests to me. "Nearly four hundred people, mostly poor Muslim students, were called in for interrogation and pressured to turn witnesses for the government in their conspiracy case. I myself was called in twice," he said. "They wanted to send a message to everyone who had challenged them, and they used the terror act because it allows you to send the harshest of messages, which is that you must remain silent in the face of all oppression."

It was a message that had been made abundantly clear in the case of the BK16.

§

After the rioting in Bhima Koregaon, rumors of a leftist conspiracy began with a complaint filed by a local businessman, a man alleging that the violence had been instigated by Maoists speaking at the Elgaar Parishad. A similar accusation was made in a report produced by the Forum for Integrated National Security, an obscure think tank composed of former military officials and headed by Seshadri Chari, an RSS man who is also a member of the BJP's national executive committee. By April 2018, the police investigations had become entirely focused on this so-called conspiracy, via a series of raids and interrogations. By June, the first group of activists, including Rona Wilson, had been arrested.

In November 2019, the BJP lost the state elections in Maharashtra. The new coalition government of Maharashtra, following up on information that the BK16 investigation had been mishandled, announced its intention to open an inquiry into the case.

The case was immediately transferred to the NIA by the central government, to which the NIA reports, burying any chance of an inquiry. The NIA is headed by YC Modi, who while unrelated to Narendra Modi, was the police officer in charge of investigations into Modi's role in the Gujarat riots when he was chief minister of the state. The panels headed by YC Modi found Modi innocent of any wrongdoing.

With the NIA now handling the Bhima Koregaon investigations, another round of arrests began. Among those detained were Gautam Navlakha (sixty-eight), a journalist and civil rights activist, and Anand Teltumbde. Hany Babu (fifty-five), a Muslim professor at Delhi University who campaigns for the rights of political prisoners, was arrested. Sagar Gorkhe (thirty-four), Ramesh Gaichor (thirty-seven) and Jyoti Jagtap (thirty-three), members of a Maharashtra-based Dalit cultural group, were also detained without bail. The conditions of their detention have aroused much concern for their safety, especially with the indifferent response of Modi's government to the COVID-19 pandemic, including to the virulent Delta variant, which was first discovered in Maharashtra.

At the height of the first wave of the pandemic, on October 8, 2020, police barged into the one-room home of eighty-three-year-old Stan Swamy in the eastern Indian city of Ranchi and took him into custody. Frail and shaking, unable to drink from a glass because of Parkinson's, Swamy had to appeal to the court after his arrest for a straw and a sipper cup. The request took nearly two months to be approved. Denied bail by a judge who argued that Swamy's "alleged sickness" was outweighed by "the collective interest of the community," Swamy was subsequently moved to a church-run hospital in May last year after complaining of COVID-19 symptoms. He remained there, under custody, until he died this July. "I knew him for over twenty years," Father

Joseph Xavier, a Jesuit priest, told me, "and to the very end, his idea of freedom was not just a matter of getting bail from the courts but to be among the indigenous people he admired, fought for and worked with all his life."

A further six of the BK16 have tested positive for COVID in jail. "There are three thousand prisoners in Taloja and not a single doctor," Jenny Rowena, Hany Babu's partner, told me. "All they have are three ayurvedic specialists, unqualified in Western medicine, who prescribe drugs." Conditions are equally bad for the three being held at Byculla women's prison—Sudha Bhardwaj, who was born in the US but gave up her American citizenship so that she could work in India as a labor activist and human rights lawyer; Shoma Sen, the literature professor, who is a Dalit and women's rights activist; and Jyoti Jagtap, the Dalit singer and activist, who was arrested by the police at a traffic light while riding to work on a motorcycle. Both groups are subject to the petty cruelties and vindictiveness rife in the prison system, with arbitrary denials of medical care, proper food, sanitary conditions, reading matter, or contact with family members and lawyers.

Shalini Gera, a colleague of Bhardwaj's and one of her legal defense team, described to me how Bhardwaj and Sen, as political prisoners, were kept in solitary cells on death row in Pune. They were allowed into a small yard for exercise, but never together. Both Bhardwaj and Sen had been attacked by mentally disturbed inmates on death row, Gera said. After Bhardwaj appealed to the courts to be allowed more than two books a month, for a while the distribution of books to prisoners had been stopped altogether in an act of retaliation.

Intimidation of those involved in the case extends beyond the prisons. Gera told me of her surprise on learning from Citizen Lab Canada, in October 2019, while she was working on Bhardwaj's defense, that her own WhatsApp account had been targeted by Pegasus. "Like most activists in India, I had always assumed that most of my emails, texts, phone calls were insecure, like everybody else's. It took some time for it to actually sink in that this was some highly sophisticated surveillance … and some VERY expensive software!!!" she told me via text message.

Neither the Pegasus findings nor the global outcry after Swamy's death has done anything to change the intimidation, surveillance, and fear of entrapment experienced by the BK16 or their supporters. A judge who expressed sadness at Swamy's death was rebuked by the NIA for affecting the morale of its officers; the judge apologized and withdrew his comments.

"All institutions have lost credibility," said Suchitra Vijayan, a New York–based writer and barrister who had been following the protests while traveling in India. "The silencing of critical voices is a core component of an authoritarian regime and that is what we can see going on here, accompanied by institutional erosion. Earlier, they never went after lawyers, but they do now. The police in India have a long history of planting evidence, but now it is done with sophisticated technology that has immense resources behind it. The judiciary has become complicit."

§

Across India, vital democratic norms are being eroded. "You should come to Uttar Pradesh and see how many people have been locked up there under sedition charges," the civil rights campaigner Nadeem Khan told me. There is a range of laws, some of them dating back to the colonial era, supplying the government with a massive toolkit of repression. When Kashmir erupted in protests after Modi unilaterally revoked its notionally autonomous status in August 2019, more than 5,000 people were imprisoned, many of them booked under a public order law specific to Kashmir.

The UAPA, however, has become the government's most valuable weapon, allowing it to suspend most fundamental rights while preserving the appearance of legality, and it is increasingly applied everywhere there is opposition to Modi. In Kashmir, there were 255 cases brought under the terror act by the end of 2019, the third-highest number among Indian states. In the northeastern state of Assam, Akhil Gogoi, a worker and peasant leader opposed to the Hindu right, was arrested on terror charges in December 2019. (Gogoi contested state elections from prison this May and won; he was released this July, the charges against him dismissed.) In August 2020, Siddique Kappan, a Muslim journalist from Kerala, was arrested under the UAPA in Uttar Pradesh while trying to report on the rape and murder of a nineteen-year-old Dalit woman. In the central Indian state of Chhattisgarh, Hidme Markam, an indigenous anti-mining activist, was arrested under the terror law this March while attending an International Women's Day event commemorating indigenous women who have been victims of state violence.

"The NIA and police are not really concerned with evidence when it comes to the UAPA, but with keeping people behind bars as long as possible." Desai, the lawyer representing the BK16, told me. "It is common for police to produce redacted witness statements, where details of the witnesses are withheld. Under UAPA, there is no way to discuss evidence during application for bail. That can happen only during the trial, and, as everyone can see, it takes years to get there," he added.

Anti-terror laws that preceded the UAPA, brutal in their own ways, nevertheless contained the provision of compensation in case of false imprisonment; with UAPA, there is none. It is possible to file a civil suit for wrongful imprisonment, Desai said, but such trials can take more than a decade in India. Most victims, as with two Muslim men who were released this June for lack of evidence after spending nine years in prison, were too afraid of being imprisoned again on false charges to risk seeking compensation in a civil suit.

If the case of the BK16 stands out, however, from India's vast ranks of political prisoners, it is for the vision of India it reveals. The case of the BK16 is not merely the Hindu right's response to the assertion of Dalit rights around the anniversary at Bhima Koregaon. It is about the Modi government seizing the opportunity to put some very troublesome opponents behind bars, people it had long ago identified as a threat because of their commitment to civil rights and equality.

The arrests had been planned and prepared for by the establishment of a massive project of surveillance, entrapment, and incarceration. That project is still alive, still picking its way stealthily through the devices of other people who have chosen to stand up against Modi's violently authoritarian version of India.

Chapter 9

The Renegade at the Nation's Gates

Arundhati Roy and the Politics of Prose

"I've always been slightly short with people who say, 'You haven't written anything again,' as if all the nonfiction I've written is not writing," Arundhati Roy said.*

It was July, and we were sitting in Roy's living room, the windows closed against the heat of the Delhi summer. Delhi might be roiled over a slowing economy, rising crimes against women, and the coming elections, but in Jor Bagh, an upscale residential area across from the sixteenth-century tombs of the Lodi Gardens, things were quiet. Roy's dog, Filthy, a stray, slept on the floor, her belly rising and falling rhythmically. The melancholy cry of a bird pierced the air. "That's a hornbill," Roy said, looking reflective.

Roy, perhaps best known for *The God of Small Things*, her novel about relationships that cross lines of caste, class, and religion, one of which leads to murder while another culminates in incest, had only recently turned again to fiction. It was another novel, but she was keeping the subject secret for now. She was

---

* First published in the *New York Times Magazine*, March 5, 2014.

still trying to shake herself free of her nearly two-decade-long role as an activist and public intellectual and spoke, with some reluctance, of one "last commitment." It was more daring than her attacks on India's occupation of Kashmir, the American wars in Iraq and Afghanistan, or crony capitalism. This time, she had taken on Mahatma Gandhi.

She'd been asked by a small Indian press, Navayana, to write an introduction to a new edition of *The Annihilation of Caste*. Written in 1936 by B. R. Ambedkar, the progressive leader who drafted the Indian constitution and converted to Buddhism, the essay is perhaps the most famous modern-day attack on India's caste system. It includes a rebuke of Gandhi, who wanted to abolish untouchability but not caste. Ambedkar saw the entire caste system as morally wrong and undemocratic. Reading Ambedkar's and Gandhi's arguments with each other, Roy became increasingly dismayed with what she saw as Gandhi's regressive position. Her small introductory essay grew larger in her mind, "almost a little book in itself." It would not pull its punches when it came to Gandhi and therefore would likely prove controversial. Even Ambedkar ran into difficulties. His views were considered so provocative that he was forced to self-publish. The more she spoke of it, the more mired in complications this last commitment of hers seemed.

Roy led me into the next room, where books and journals were scattered around the kitchen table that serves as her desk. The collected writings of Ambedkar and Gandhi, voluminous and in combat with each other, sat in towering stacks, bookmarks tucked between the pages. The notebook in which Roy had been jotting down her thoughts in small, precise handwriting lay open on the table, a fragile intermediary in a nearly century-old debate between giants.

"I got into trouble in the past for my nonfiction," Roy said, "and I swore, 'I'm never going to write anything with a footnote again.'" It's a promise she has so far been unable to keep. "I've been gathering the thoughts for months, struggling with the questions, shocked by what I've been reading," she said, when I asked if she had begun the essay. "I know that when it comes out, a lot is going to happen. But it's something I need to do."

§

In her late thirties, Roy was perhaps India's most famous writer. The publication of *The God of Small Things* in 1997 coincided with the fiftieth anniversary of India's independence. It was the beginning of an aggressively nationalist, consumerist phase, and Roy was seen as representative of Brand India. The novel, her first, appeared on the *New York Times* best-seller list and won the Booker Prize. It went on to sell more than 6 million copies. British tabloids published bewildering profiles ("A 500,000-pound book from the pickle-factory outcast"), while magazines photographed her—all cascading waves of hair and high cheekbones—against the pristine waterways and lush foliage of Kerala, where the novel was set and which was just beginning to take off as a tourist destination.

Roy's tenure as a national icon came to an abrupt end when, a year later, the Hindu right-wing BJP government carried out a series of nuclear tests. These were widely applauded by Indians who identified with Hindu nationalism, many of them members of the rising middle class. In an essay titled "The End of Imagination," Roy accused supporters of the tests of reveling in displays of military power—embracing the jingoism that had brought the BJP to power for only the second time since independence—instead of addressing the abysmal conditions in which a majority of Indians lived. Published simultaneously in the English-language magazines *Outlook* and *Frontline*, the essay marked her beginning as an overtly political writer.

§

Roy's political turn angered many in her upper-caste, urban, English-speaking audience, even as it attracted another set of readers. Most of her new fans had never heard of her novel; they often spoke languages other than English and felt marginalized because of their religion, caste, or ethnicity, left behind by India's economic rise. They devoured the essays Roy began writing, which were distributed in unauthorized translations, and flocked to rallies to hear her speak. "There was all this resentment, quite understandable, about *The God of Small Things*, that here was this person writing in English winning all this money," Roy said. "So when 'The End of Imagination' came out, there was a reversal, an anger among the English-speaking people, but also an embrace from everyone else."

The vehemence of the response surprised her. "There is nothing in *The God of Small Things* that is at odds with what I went on to write politically over fifteen years," Roy said. "It's instinctive territory." It is true that her novel also explored questions of social justice. But without the armature of character and plot, her essays seemed didactic—or just plain wrong—to her detractors, easy stabs at an India full of energy and purpose. Even those who sympathized with her views were often suspicious of her celebrity, regarding her as a dilettante. But for Roy, remaining on the sidelines was never an option. "If I had not said anything about the nuclear tests, it would have been as if I was celebrating it," Roy said. "I was on the covers of all these magazines all the time. Not saying anything became as political as saying something."

Roy turned next to a series of mega-dams to be built on the Narmada River. Villagers likely to be displaced by the project had been staging protests, even as India's Supreme Court allowed construction to go forward. Roy traveled through the region, joining in the protests and writing essays criticizing the court's decision. In 2001, a group of men accused her and other activists of attacking them at a rally outside the Supreme Court. Roy petitioned for the charges to be dismissed. The court agreed but was so offended by the language of her petition (she accused the court of attempting to "muzzle dissent, to harass and intimidate those who disagree with it") that it held her in contempt. "Showing the magnanimity of law by keeping in mind that the respondent is a woman," the judgment read, "and hoping that better sense and wisdom shall dawn upon the respondent in the future to serve the cause of art and literature," Roy was to be sentenced to "simple imprisonment for one day" and a fine of 2,000 rupees.

The 2002 BBC documentary *DAM/AGE* captures some of the drama around Roy's imprisonment at the fortresslike Tihar Jail. When she emerged the next day, her transformation from Indian icon to harsh national critic was complete. Her hair, which she had shorn into a severe cut, evoked, uneasily, both ostracized woman and feisty feminist. The English-language Indian media mocked Roy for criticizing the dams, which they saw as further evidence of India's rise. Attacks followed each of her subsequent works: her anguished denunciations of the massacre of Muslims in Gujarat in 2002; the plans for bauxite mining in Orissa (now Odisha) by a London-based corporation called Vedanta Resources; the paramilitary operations in central India against indigenous tribal populations and ultraleft guerrillas known as Naxalites; and India's military presence in Kashmir, where more than a half million troops hold in check a majority Muslim population that wants to secede from India.

Kashmir, over which India has fought three of its four wars against Pakistan, would become one of Roy's defining issues. In 2010, after a series of massive protests during which teenage boys faced off against soldiers, Roy publicly remarked that

"Kashmir was never an integral part of India." In suggesting that the state of India was a mere construct, a product of partition like Pakistan, she had crossed a line. Most progressives in India haven't gone that far. Roy soon found herself the center of a nationwide storm. A stone-throwing mob, trailed by television vans, showed up at her front door. The conservative TV channel Times Now ran slow-motion clips of her visiting Kashmir in which she looked as if she were sashaying down a catwalk, refusing to answer a reporter's questions. Back in Delhi, Times Now convened a panel moderated by its immensely popular host, Arnab Goswami, to discuss—squeezed between headlines and a news crawl in which "anger" and "Arundhati" were the most common words—whether Roy should be arrested for sedition. When the sole Kashmiri Muslim panelist, Hameeda Nayeem, pointed out that Roy had said nothing not already believed by a majority of Kashmiris, she was cut off by Goswami. Cases were filed against Roy in courts in Bangalore and Chandigarh, accusing her of being "antinational," "anti-human" and supposedly writing in one of her essays that "Kashmir should get freedom from naked, starving Indians."

§

The apartment where I met Roy in July occupies the topmost floor of a three-story house and has all the trappings of an upper-class home—a sprawl of surrounding lawn, a high fence, and a small elevator. There are few signs of her dissenter status: the stickers on her door ("We have to be very careful these days because …"); the books in the living room (Howard Zinn, Noam Chomsky, Eduardo Galeano); and, particularly unusual in the Indian context, the absence of servants (Roy lives entirely alone). Perhaps what is most telling is how Roy ended up in this house, which she used to ride past every day on her way to work, on a bicycle rented for a rupee.

Roy was born Suzanna Arundhati Roy in 1959 in Shillong, a small hill town in the northeastern fringes of India. Her mother, Mary, was from a close-knit community of Syrian Christians in Kerala. Her father, Rajib, was a Bengali Hindu from Calcutta, a manager of a tea plantation near Shillong, and an alcoholic. The marriage didn't last long, and when Roy was two, she and her brother, Lalith, a year and a half older, returned to Kerala with their mother. Unwelcome at the family home, they moved into a cottage owned by Roy's maternal grandfather in Ooty, in the neighboring state of Tamil Nadu.

"Then there are a lot of horrible stories," Roy said and began to laugh. "My mother was very ill, a severe asthmatic. We thought she was dying. She would send us into town with a basket, and the shopkeepers would put food in the basket, mostly just rice with green chilies." The family remained there until Roy was five, defying attempts by her grandmother and uncle to turn them out of the house (inheritance laws among Syrian Christians heavily favored sons). Eventually, Roy's mother moved back to Kerala and started a school on the premises of the local Rotary Club.

As the child of a single mother, Roy was ill at ease in the conservative Syrian Christian community. She felt more at home among the so-called lower castes or Dalits, who were kept at a distance by both Christians and upper-caste Hindus.

"Much of the way I think is by default," she said. "Nobody paid enough attention to me to indoctrinate me." By the time she was sent to Lawrence, a boarding school founded by a British Army officer (motto: "Never Give In"), it was perhaps too late for indoctrination. Roy, who was ten, says the only thing she remembers about Lawrence was becoming obsessed with running. Her brother, who heads a seafood-export business in Kerala, recalls her time there differently. "When she was in middle school, she was quite popular among the senior boys," he told me, laughing. "She was also a prefect and a tremendous debater."

Roy concedes that boarding school had its uses. "It made it easier to light out when I did," she said. The child of what was considered a disreputable marriage and an even more disgraceful divorce, Roy was expected to have suitably modest ambitions. Her future prospects were summed up by the first college she was placed in; it was run by nuns and offered secretarial training. At sixteen, Roy instead moved to Delhi to study at the School of Planning and Architecture.

Roy chose architecture because it would allow her to start earning money in her second year, but also out of idealism. In Kerala, she met the British-born Indian architect Laurie Baker, known for his sustainable, low-cost buildings, and was taken with the idea of doing similar work. But she soon realized she wouldn't learn about such things at school. "They just wanted you to be like a contractor," Roy said, still indignant. She was grappling, she said, with questions to which her professors didn't seem to have answers: "What is your sense of aesthetic? Whom are you designing for? Even if you're designing a home, what is the relationship between men and women assumed in that? It just became bigger and bigger. How are cities organized? Who are laws for? Who is considered a citizen? This coalesced into something very political for me by the end of it."

For her final project, Roy refused to design a building and instead wrote a thesis, "Postcolonial Urban Development in Delhi." "I said: 'Now I want to tell you what I've learned here. I don't want you to tell me what I've learned here.'" Roy drew sustenance from the counterculture that existed among her fellow students, which she would represent years later in the film *In Which Annie Gives*

It Those Ones (1989). She wrote, designed, and appeared in it—an elfin figure with a giant Afro playing the character of Radha, who gives up architecture to become a writer but drowns before completing her first novel.

By this time, Roy had broken off contact with her family. Without money to stay in the student hostel, she moved into a nearby slum with her boyfriend, Gerard da Cunha. (They pretended to be married in deference to the slum's conservative mores.) "It's one thing to be a young person who decides to slum it," Roy said. "For me, it wasn't like that. There was nobody. There was no cuteness about it. That was my university, that period when you think from the point of view of absolute vulnerability. And that hasn't left me."

After graduation, she briefly lived with Da Cunha, in Goa, where he was from, but they broke up, and she returned to Delhi. She got a job at the National Institute of Urban Affairs, and met Pradip Krishen, an independent filmmaker who offered Roy the female lead in *Massey Sahib* (1985), a film set in colonial India in which Roy played a goatherd. Roy and Krishen, who later married, collaborated on subsequent projects, including "Bargad," a twenty-six-part television series on India's independence movement that was never completed, as well as two feature films, *Annie* and *Electric Moon* (1992).

Krishen's background could not have been more different from Roy's. A Balliol scholar and former history professor, Krishen, a widower, lived with his parents and two children in a sprawling house in the posh Chanakyapuri neighborhood. When Roy joined him, they moved to a separate apartment upstairs. Roy immersed herself in Delhi's independent-filmmaking world. The movies' progressive themes appealed to her, but it was a world dominated by the scions of elite families, and it soon came to seem out of touch and insular to her. She spent more and more time teaching aerobics, to earn her own money, and hanging out with artists she met in school.

She had already begun work on her novel when *Bandit Queen*, a film based on the life of the female bandit Phoolan Devi, was released. Devi was a low-caste woman who became a famous gang leader and endured gang rape and imprisonment. Roy was incensed by the way the film portrayed her as a victim whose life was defined by rape instead of rebellion. "When I saw the film, I was infuriated, partly because I had grown up in Kerala, being taken to these Malayalam films, where in every film—every film—a woman got raped," Roy said. "For many years, I believed that all women got raped. Then I read in the papers how Phoolan Devi said it was like being raped again. I read the book the film was based on and realized that these guys had added their own rapes … I thought, You've changed India's most famous bandit into history's most famous rape victim." Roy's essay on the film, "The Great Indian Rape Trick," published in the now-defunct *Sunday* magazine, eviscerated the makers of *Bandit Queen*, pointing out that they never even bothered to meet Phoolan Devi or to invite her to a screening.

The piece alienated many of the people Roy worked with. Krishen, who gives the impression of a flinty loyalty toward Roy even though the couple split up, says it was seen as a betrayal in the tight-knit film circles of Delhi. For Roy, it was a lesson in how the media worked. "I watched very carefully what happened to Phoolan Devi," she said. "I saw how the media can just excavate you and leave a shell behind. And I was lucky to learn from that. So when my turn came, the barricades were up."

§

When I met Roy at the New Delhi airport a few days after we first talked, she hung back from the crowd, ignoring the stares coming her way. She had turned down a request to address a public gathering in Kashmir, but there still seemed something political about traveling there just a week after eight Indian soldiers were killed in an ambush. The passengers on the flight Roy and I took, Hindu pilgrims visiting the Amarnath shrine, certainly thought so. Periodically, they filled the small aircraft with cries of "Bom Bhole," or "Hail Shiva," their right fists rising in unison. Once in Srinagar, the capital, Roy was stopped often by Kashmiris who wanted to thank her for speaking up against the Indian state. They also hoped she would agree to have her picture taken with them. She usually did.

But for the most part, she kept out of the public eye. Roy was staying at the house of a journalist friend, and as he and another journalist talked on their mobile phones, following a story about a fight that had broken out between Amarnath pilgrims and Kashmiri porters, she distributed packs of Lavazza coffee brought from Delhi, only half listening. Later, she declined to attend the screening of a new documentary about the Naxalite guerrillas, preferring to work on her novel.

Roy had come to Kashmir mainly to see friends, but it was hard to escape the strife altogether. A few days later, we drove through the countryside, a landscape of streams sparkling through green fields and over cobblestones, punctuated by camouflaged, gun-toting figures. Sometimes they were a detachment of the Central Reserve Police Force, sometimes the local police and, every now and then, distinctive in their flat headgear, soldiers of the counterinsurgency Rashtriya Rifles. "There were bunkers all over Srinagar when I first began coming here," Roy said. "Now they use electronic surveillance for the city. The overt policing is for the countryside."

In Srinagar earlier that week, the policing had seemed overt enough. Roy had been invited to speak at a gathering organized by Khurram Parvez,* who works for the Jammu and Kashmir Coalition of Civil Society, an organization that has produced extensive reports on mass graves and extrajudicial killings in Kashmir. As forty or so people sat cross-legged on the floor—activists, lawyers, journalists, and students—Parvez asked that cell phones be turned off and placed in "thighland" in order to prevent surreptitious recordings that could be passed on to authorities.

Roy put on reading glasses, and these, along with the stack of books in front of her, a selection of the nonfiction she has written over the past fifteen years (just brought out by Penguin India as a box set of five candy-colored volumes), gave the gathering the air of an impromptu seminar. Roy began by asking audience members to discuss what was on their minds. A young lawyer who grew up in a village about thirty miles from Srinagar told a story of two women, who, after being raped by soldiers, spent the night shivering in separate bathing cabins, too ashamed to go home, hearing only each other's weeping. Roy listened carefully to this and similar accounts, occasionally nudging the conversation beyond Kashmir, to the rifts and fractures within India itself, including the forests of central India, where she spent more than two weeks in 2010 with ultraleft guerrillas and their tribal allies for her last book, *Broken Republic* (2011).

"I feel sad, you know, when I'm traveling in India and see Kashmiris who've been recruited into the Border Security Force," she said. "It's what this state does, hiring from one part of the country and sending them to fight in other parts, against people

---

* Parvez, who was detained at the Delhi airport in 2016, as he was on his way to attend a United Nations Human Rights Council session in Geneva, has been arrested and incarcerated multiple times. In November 2021, he was arrested by the NIA and charged under the UAPA. He remains in prison.

who on the surface might seem different but who are actually facing the same kind of oppression, and this is why perhaps it's important to be able to talk to each other."

She picked up one of the books in front of her, the lemon-yellow *Listening to Grasshoppers*, and found a passage from the essay "Azadi," or "Freedom." In it, she describes attending a 2008 rally in Srinagar demanding independence from India. "The slogan that cut through me like a knife," she read in a quiet, clear voice, "was this one: *Nanga bhooka Hindustan, jaan se pyaara Pakistan*"— India is a naked, starving country; Pakistan is more precious to us than life itself. "In that slogan," she said, "I saw the seeds of how easily victims can become perpetrators."

The discussion went on for hours, spanning global capitalism and climate change, before returning to Kashmir. Did Kashmiris identify with Pakistan? Some did, some emphatically did not. What about the role of women in the struggle for Kashmiri self-determination? How could they make themselves heard when they found it so difficult to make themselves heard in this room? In the fierce summer heat, the group splintered into factions, growing tired and agitated. Roy decided to bring the proceedings to a close with a joke from Monty Python's *Life of Brian*.

"In the movie, this man, Brian, asks a band of guerrilla fighters, 'Are you the Judean Peoples' Front?'" Roy said, mimicking a British accent. "And the reply he gets from this really offended group is: No, absolutely not. 'We're the Peoples' Front of Judea.'" The joke, an elaborate parody of radical factionalism, made Roy laugh heartily. It also changed the emotional temperature of the room. As we came out of the house and milled around in the alley, the various groups seemed easier with each other. Later, a young man who had just completed a degree in fiction would express to me his disappointment that the conversation had never turned to novels at all.

§

Beyond the Gandhi book, there has been much to pull Roy away from fiction. In May, when Naxalite guerrillas killed at least twenty-four people, including a Congress politician who had formed a brutal right-wing militia and whom Roy criticized in her last book, she was immediately asked for a comment. She refused to say anything. "So they just republished an old interview I had given and tried to pretend it was a new interview," she said.

"The things I've needed to say directly, I've said already," she said. "Now I feel like I would be repeating myself with different details." We were sitting in her living room, and she paused, knowing the next question would be how political her new fiction would be. "I'm not a person who likes to use fiction as a means. I think it's an irreducible thing, fiction. It's itself. It's not a movie, it's not a political tract, it's not a slogan. The ways in which I have thought politically, the proteins of that have to be broken down and forgotten about, until it comes out as the sweat on your skin."

But publishing is a risky venture in India these days; court orders are used to prevent books from coming out or to remove them from circulation, even when they are not explicitly political. Most recently, Penguin India pulped all existing copies of *The Hindus: An Alternative History* by Wendy Doniger, after a conservative Hindu pressure group initiated a case against the book. Penguin also publishes Roy, and she felt compelled to protest.

Although Roy won't divulge, even to her closest friends, what her new novel is about, she is adamant that it represents a break from both her nonfiction and her first novel. "I'm not trying to write *The God of Small Things* again," she said. "There's much more grappling conceptually with the new novel. It is much easier for a book about a family—which is what *The God of Small Things* was— to have a clear emotional heart." Before she became caught up in her essay on Ambedkar and Gandhi, she was working on the novel by drawing, as she tends to do in the early stages, trying to figure out the structure. She then writes longhand. What she calls the "sandpapering" takes place on a laptop, at her kitchen table.

"I'm not attached to any particular space," she said when I asked her how important the routine was to her writing. "I just don't need to feel that someone's breathing over me."

After *The God of Small Things* was published, she began to give away some of the money she had made from it. She sent her father, who resurfaced after she appeared in *Massey Sahib* and was not above trying to extort money from her, to a rehab center. (He died in 2007.) In 2002, when Roy received a Lannan Foundation award, she donated the $350,000 prize money to fifty small organizations around India. Finally, in 2006, she and her friends set up a trust into which she began putting all her nonfiction earnings to support progressive causes around the country.

"I was never interested in just being a professional writer where you wrote one book that did very well, you wrote another book, and so on," Roy said, thinking of the ways in which *The God of Small Things* trapped her and freed her. "There's a fear that I have, that because you're famous, or because you've done something, everybody wants you to keep on doing the same thing, be the same person, freeze you in time." Roy was talking of the point in her life when, tired of the images she saw of herself—the glamorous Indian icon turned glamorous Indian dissenter—she cut off her hair. But you could see how she might say the same of the position in which she now finds herself. The essay on Gandhi and Ambedkar was meant to complete one set of expectations before she could turn to something new. "I don't want that enormous baggage," Roy said. "I want to travel light."

Acknowledgments

These pieces would not have been possible without the vision and support of Sheila Glaser at the *New York Times Magazine*, Clare Longrigg and David Wolf at the *Guardian*, Theodore Ross and Gabriel Snyder at the *New Republic*, David Samuels at *Tablet Magazine*, John Summers at *The Baffler*, and Jennifer Szalai at *Harper's*. I remain grateful to them for being such wonderful editors and for allowing me to pursue difficult stories running counter to the received myths about India as a flourishing democracy.

§

I am grateful to all my fact-checkers and their dedication to the truth. They made me feel a sense of shared purpose, and their immense labor has much to do with the great pride I feel in these pieces. Thank you to Aaron Braun ("Impossible Machines"), Noah Hurowitz ("Killing Gauri Lankesh"), Karen Fragala-Smith ("The Renegade at the Nation's Gates"), Lindsey Gilbert ("An Alien Visitation"), Laura Reston ("Nowhere Man"), Theodore Ross ("Nowhere Land"), and Steven Stern and Bill Vourvoulias ("Manufacturing Foreigners").

§

My gratitude to the following people, many of them in India, who shared, variously, advice, contacts, thoughts, facts, meals, drinks, camaraderie, and companionship on reporting trips: Ratik Asokan, Adil Bhat, Hartosh Singh Bal, Kishalay Bhattacharjee, Radhika Bordia, Seema Chishti, Kushanava Chowdhury, Atul Dev, Jaskiran Dhillon, Scharada Dubey, Sujatha Gidla, Dr Marwan Jallad, Dhirendra Jha, Vinod Jose, Sanjay Kak, Malav Kanuga, Mary Therese Kurkalang, Jinendra Maibam, Pankaj Mishra, Sadiq Naqvi, Vivek Narayanan, Arundhati Roy, Arunabh Saikia, Abhijit Saha, Arijit Sen, Krishna Pratap Singh, Valay Singh, and Makepeace Sitlhou. There are many others whose friendship and help I am grateful for, but who must remain anonymous for reasons of safety.

§

I am grateful to Andy Hsiao for championing this book from beginning to end, to Anthony Arnove for making it possible, and to everyone at Haymarket for bringing it into the world.

§

As always, I owe the most to Ranen (aka the Bear) for encouragement, inspiration, laughs, and for simply being there.

Previously Published

Deb, Siddhartha. "New Face of India: The Anti-Gandhi Movement." *New Republic*. May 3, 2016. https://newrepublic.com/article/133014/new-face-india-anti-gandhi.

Deb, Siddhartha. "Worst Industrial Disaster in the History of the World." *The Baffler*. October 2014. https://thebaffler.com/salvos/worst-industrial-disaster-history-world.

Deb, Siddhartha. "Nowhere Land: Along India's Border, a Forgotten Burmese Rebellion." *Harper's Magazine*, January 2009.

Deb, Siddhartha. "They Are Manufacturing Foreigners": How India Disenfranchises Muslims." *New York Times Magazine*. September 15, 2021. https://www.nytimes.com/2021/09/15/magazine/india-assam-muslims.html.

Deb, Siddhartha. "The Idol and the Mosque." *Tablet Magazine*. April 6, 2022. https://www.tabletmag.com/sections/news/articles/the-idol-and-the-mosque.

Deb, Siddhartha. "Those Mythological Men and Their Sacred Supersonic Flying Temples." *New Republic*. May 14, 2015. https://newrepublic.com/article/121792/those-mythological-men-and-their-sacred-supersonic-flying-temples.

Deb, Siddhartha. "The Killing of Gauri Lankesh." *Columbia Journalism Review*. February 15, 2018. https://www.cjr.org/special_report/gauri-lankesh-killing.php.

Deb, Siddhartha. "The Unravelling of a Conspiracy: Were the 16 Charged with Plotting to Kill India's Prime Minister Framed?" *Guardian*. August 12, 2021. https://www.theguardian.com/world/2021/aug/12/bhima-koregaon-case-india-conspiracy-modi.

Deb, Siddhartha. "Arundhati Roy: The Not-So-Reluctant Renegade." *New York Times Magazine*. March 5, 2014. https://www.nytimes.com/2014/03/09/magazine/arundhati-roy-the-not-so-reluctant-renegade.html.

Index

Page numbers followed by an *n* refer to footnotes.

2002 Gujarat massacres: investigations into, 26–29; Muslims blamed for, 24, 116; Narendra Modi's response to, 24–25, 38–39; public response to, 25; train fire that precipitated, 23, 116; as unusual, 24

Adani, Gautam, 31
Advani, L. K., 22, 113
Allahabad, disappearance of, 1–2
All Burma Students' Democratic Front (ABSDF), 76
ancient India: complexity of, 140–141; general timeline of, 140; Hindu right's paradisiacal view of, 141, 152–154
"Ancient Indian Aviation Technology" (Bodas, Jadhav), 139–140
Anil, 114–116, 126–127, 130, 136–137
Annihilation of Caste, The (Ambedkar), 192
anxiety of imitation, 148–149
Armed Forces Special Powers Act, 65, 96
Arsenal Consulting, 180–182
Assam: attacks against Bengali Muslims in, 93; detention centers in, 98, 106; multiethnic society of, 90, 93, 95–96; protests against Citizenship Amendment Act (CAA), 98–99; role of British colonization in, 95–96
Assam agitation, 96
Assamese nationalism, 95, 97, 105
Ayodhya, Ram temple: 2019 Supreme Court judgment on, 117, 120–121; archaeological digs regarding, 118–120; global nature of campaign to build, 22, 112–113, 117; involvement of monks in, 132, 134; Islamophobia inherent in campaign to build, 22–23, 116–117; model of, 108–109, 127; Narendra Modi's role in campaign to build, 3, 22, 113, 117, 120; temporary set-up of, 131
Ayodhya, Ram temple construction: as central to Hindu nationalist mythology, 108; controversies regarding, 126; impact on Ayodhya of, 116–117, 136–137

Babri Masjid: 1992 destruction of, 22; 113–114, 128; Ram idol inside, 112
"Banned in Benares" (Deb), 3–4

211

Beautiful and the Damned, The (Deb), 4–5

Bharatiya Janata Party (BJP): in Assam, 97–98, 105; citizens rendered stateless by, 89–91, 103–104; development of, 111–112; and Lingayats, 163; relationship with Rashtriya Swayamsevak Sangh (RSS), 21, 111–112; response to anti-CAA and NRC protests by, 99; support of Burmese junta by, 64, 69. *See also* Hindu nationalism; Rashtriya Swayamsevak Sangh (RSS)

Bharatiya Janata Party (BJP), elections: 1998 historic win, 15, 23; 2014 win, 5, 22, 117, 157, 170; 2019 win, 3, 5, 99, 117; 2022 campaign in Uttar Pradesh, 121–122; assassinations in lead up to, 157, 163, 166; Ayodhya temple-building campaign's impact on, 113–114

Bhardwaj, Sudha, 178, 187

Bhima Koregaon conspiracy, 176–177, 185. *See also* BK16

Bhopal, 1984 industrial disaster: cause of, 53; chronic health conditions and disabilities caused by, 47–48, 54; community response to, 54–55, 59–60; criminal case regarding, 56–57; deaths caused by, 47; experience of, 50n; government's response to, 55; Indian elite's response to, 58–59; present-day impacts of, 54; release of methyl isocyanate (MIC) during, 46; role of factory safety measures in, 51–53; trial regarding, 55–56; as worst in world history, 7, 45. *See also* Dow Chemical Company

Bhopal Gas Peedit Mahila Udyog Sangathan, 55

Bhopal Group for Information and Action, 55

"Bhopal: Unending Disaster, Enduring Resistance" (Hanna), 51n

BK16: activism by, 176, 178; arrests of, 178, 186; case as representative of the Modi government, 190; COVID-19 pandemic and, 178, 186–187; government's case against, 179–181; incarceration without bail of, 7, 178–179, 187; Maharashtra government's inquiry into case against, 185–186; manufactured evidence against, 180–182; targeting of associates of, 181, 187–188

books, destruction of, 149, 204

British colonization, 95–96, 109

Burmese democracy, 84n

Burmese dissidents: guerrilla army planned by, 76–77; Indian government's original support of, 76; Indian government's present-day response to, 62, 78–79; and Manipuri insurgents, 76–77; Manipuri life of, 77–78; and Trans-Asian Highway, 82. *See also* Leikun refugee camp

capitalism. *See* global capitalism

carbaryl. *See* Sevin

Central Bureau of Investigation (CBI): and Bhopal 1984 industrial disaster, 57; and Hindu right assassinations, 164–165; raids led by, 39, 168

Citizen Lab Canada, 181

Citizens for Justice and Peace (CJP), 26

citizenship, determined by: Assamese voter records, 92;

Citizenship Amendment Act (CAA), 91; foreigners' tribunals, 87, 90, 92; National Register of Citizens (NRC), 90, 92
Citizenship Amendment Act (CAA): arrests of protesters against, 184–185; comparison to Nazi Germany's Reich Citizens Law, 89; intentional targeting of Muslims by, 3, 89, 91; protests against, 98–99, 183. *See also* National Register of Citizens (NRC)
cows, protection of, 110, 149

Dabholkar, Narendra, 162, 164
DAM/AGE (2002), 195
Das, Dinendra, 132–133
detention centers, 98, 106
Dow Chemical Company: Indian elite's courting of, 59; insistence of no connection to Bhopal by, 56; napalm manufacturing by, 49. *See also* Bhopal, 1984 industrial disaster; Union Carbide
"Dulce et Decorum est" (Owen), 50n
D voters, 92

"End of Imagination, The" (Roy), 193–194
extrajudicial executions. *See* Hindu right assassinations

foreigners' tribunals: and burden of proof, 92; creation of, 92; cycle of poverty perpetuated by, 101–102; disproportionate impact on women of, 87–88, 94; and National Register of Citizens (NRC), 90, 92, 98. *See also* Citizenship Amendment Act (CAA)

Gauri Lankesh Patrike, 161–162, 171. *See also* Lankesh, Gauri, work
global capitalism: as distraction, 8, 32; and Hindu nationalism, 2–5, 8, 14–15, 25–26
global war on terror. *See* war on terror
God of Small Things, The (Roy), 191, 193–194
Gogoi, Ranjan, 97, 120
Gohain, Hiren, 103–104
Golwalkar, M. S., 19, 111
"Great Indian Rape Trick, The" (Roy), 200
Green Revolution, 49
Gujarat government: targeting of Ashis Nandy by, 38; targeting of Teesta Setalvad by, 39; as vigilante-police state, 27–29. *See also* resistance to Hindu nationalism
Gujarat massacres. *See* 2002 Gujarat massacres
Gujarat model, 29–32

Hanuman, 129
Hindu nationalism: and Assamese nationalism, 95, 97, 105; caste system maintained by, 16–17; development of, 18–19, 89, 111; national media's complacence with, 168–169; projection of India by, 33; as successful right-wing phenomenon, 2; technology's role in, 14, 17–18; and war on terror, 4, 177, 179; Western allyship with, 4. *See also* Bharatiya Janata Party (BJP); Rashtriya Swayamsevak Sangh (RSS)
Hindu nationalism, followers: insecurity of, 16–17, 20, 41–42; rage of, 17–18, 27, 41–43; and Rashtriya Muslim Manch, 115, 123; violence against Dalits of,

40, 177; violence against Muslims of, 22–24, 36–37, 93, 96, 116–117; violence against opposition of, 41, 183
Hindu nationalism, linguistics: and declarations of victory, 14, 18, 42–43, 124; and slogans, 22, 43; as tool of erasure, 1–2; used to incite anti-Muslim violence, 25, 37, 90, 105; used to incite violence against opposition, 37, 39, 43, 170
Hindu nationalism, mythmaking: and ancient India, 140–141, 152–154; and citizenship, 87–91, 93; and Hanuman, 129–130; and Ram, 108, 112–113, 118–120, 125, 137–138; success of, 2–3; and vimanas, 150–152
Hindu nationalism, visual cues: Islamophobic mural as, 125; saffron clothing as, 14, 16, 117; Vivekananda's posture as, 18–19
Hindu right assassinations: and attacks on journalists, 166–167; characteristics of, 165–166; and extrajudicial executions, 27, 96, 161; of Hindutva critics, 159, 162, 167–168; limited investigations into, 164–166; national media's limited coverage of, 168–169. *See also* Lankesh, Gauri, assassination; resistance to Hindu nationalism
Hindus: An Alternative History, The (Doniger), 149
Hindutva, 22, 157–158, 171–172
Holy Cow: Beef in Indian Dietary Traditions (Jha), 4

India, contradictions of present-day, 14–15, 30–33, 107–110, 136–138, 148–149

India and Pakistan, creation of, 96, 111
Indian diaspora, 13–18, 30, 32–33, 41–42, 148–149. *See also* Ayodhya, Ram temple
Indian Supreme Court: and Ayodhya Ram temple, 117, 120–121; and Bhopal 1984 industrial disaster, 57; and Narendra Modi, 25–27; and National Register of Citizens (NRC), 88, 97–98, 103, 106
In Which Annie Gives It Those Ones (Roy), 199
Islamophobia: and erasure of Muslims, 1–2, 137–138, 152–153; and war on terror, 4, 27–28, 38, 185; weaponized by Hindu right, 22–24, 36–38, 96–97, 104–105, 116–117

Jammu and Kashmir Coalition of Civil Society, 202
Josyer, G. R., 143–144
journalism, dangers of, 157–158
Jyotipunj (Modi), 20–21

Kalburgi, M. M., 161–163
Kashmir: Arundhati Roy's support of, 195–196; attacks on journalists in, 166; constitutional status of, 3, 188; government repression in, 166, 188; and self-determination, 203; as threat to Hindu right, 89; and Unlawful Activities Prevention Act (UAPA), 189
Khatun, Sahera, 87–89
Ko Thein, 75–79
Ko Todu, 75–79
Kumar, Kanhaiya, 40

Lal, Hazari, 127–128

Lankesh, Gauri: financial strain experienced by, 169; opposition to Hindu nationalism by, 163; as targeted for her politics, 170
Lankesh, Gauri, assassination: description of, 157; by Hindu right, 164, 172–173; investigations into, 163, 172; other murders similar to, 162–164; public response to, 158, 170
Lankesh, Gauri, work, 159–162
Leikun refugee camp: description of, 80–81; isolation of, 79–80, 84; and Manipur Rifles camp, 80–82, 84; treatment of people in, 82; village chief of, 81. *See also* Burmese dissidents
Light at the End of the World, The (Deb), 8
Lingayats, 163–164
Listening to Grasshoppers (Roy), 203
Look East policy, 62–63, 70

Make in India, 14, 31
Malhotra, Rajiv, 34–35
Manipur: border with Burma, 7, 61–62, 69–71; ethnic clashes in, 65n; insurgent groups in, 65–66, 68, 76–77; narcotics trade in, 72
Maoists, 161
methyl isocyanate (MIC), 46, 50. *See also* Bhopal, 1984 industrial disaster; Sevin
Mishra, Pankaj, 4
Miya poets, 100–101
model minority, 4, 33
Modi, Narendra: early life of, 14, 20; as embodiment of Hindu nationalism, 3, 14; as fascist, 38–39; as responsible for 2002 massacres, 8, 25–27, 34; self-aggrandizement by, 15–16, 36, 41; wife of, 37
Modi, Narendra, rise of: and 2014 "presidential" electoral campaign, 35–36, 39, 97; and Rashtriya Swayamsevak Sangh (RSS), 20–22, 113; role in Gujarat government, 23, 27–29; role of Indian Americans in, 33–35; role of Islamophobia in, 32, 36–37, 97, 117; role of the West in, 5–6, 13–15, 29–30, 35–36, 41
Moreh: border with Tamu, 70–71; Burmese dissidents in, 68–69; description of, 61
Myth of the Holy Cow, The (Jha), 149
mythology. *See* Hindu nationalism, mythmaking

Nandy, Ashis, 37–38
Narayan, 68–69
National Investigation Agency: and BK16, 179–180, 182, 186, 188; role in Hindu right assassinations of, 164–165
National Register of Citizens (NRC): and burden of proof, 90, 92, 98; as central to Bharatiya Janata Party (BJP) in Assam, 89, 97–98; cost of, 102; creation of, 90–91; and foreigners' tribunals, 92; and objection letters, 98; proposals for those declared foreigners by, 103–104; suicides caused by, 90, 102; targeting of Muslims by, 90–91. *See also* Citizenship Amendment Act (CAA)
Naxalites, 161, 204
Ney Myo, 81–84
Nirmohi *akhara*, 132–134

northeastern India: characteristics of, 65; checkpoints in, 67, 70–71. *See also* Manipur

Orientalism (Said), 5

Pandya, Haren, 28
Pansare, Govind, 162, 164
Pegasus spyware, 181–182, 187–188
pesticides, 49
political assassinations. *See* Hindu right assassinations
Prayagraj. *See* Allahabad, disappearance of
pride of wealth, 24
Purushottam Ram, 134–135

"Race Spirit," 19, 111
Ramayana, 108, 135
Ram Lalla, 131, 134
Ramrajya, 108, 125
Ram temple. *See* Ayodhya, Ram temple
Rashtriya Muslim Manch, 115, 123
Rashtriya Swayamsevak Sangh (RSS): Hindu "Race Spirit" developed by, 19–20, 111; Hindutva philosophy of, 22; involvement in assassinations by, 159, 168; Narendra Modi's involvement in, 20–22, 113; recruitment strategies of, 111; relationship with Bharatiya Janata Party (BJP), 21, 111–112; role in 1984 pogrom against Sikh minority of, 21. *See also* Bharatiya Janata Party (BJP); Hindu nationalism
resistance to Hindu nationalism: journalism's role in, 157–158, 162, 166–169, 171; manufactured evidence against, 180–182, 184–185; Pegasus spyware targeting, 181–182, 187–188; Unlawful Activities Prevention Act (UAPA) used to repress, 189. *See also* Gujarat government; Hindu right assassinations

Roy, Arundhati: criminal contempt notice issued to, 40; criticisms of Hindu nationalism by, 4, 7–8, 193, 202–204; criticisms of Mahatma Gandhi by, 192; focus on Kashmir by, 195–196; freedom desired by, 2005; imprisonment of, 195; influence of Bandit Queen on, 200; as national icon, 193; national media's attacks on, 196; privacy of, 201
Roy, Arundhati, early life: childhood, 197–198; college education, 198–199; filmmaking, 199–200
Roy, Arundhati, writing: criticisms of, 195; earnings from, 205; fiction, 191–192; public response to, 194

Sahera Khatun v. the Union of India, 88, 106n
Sanatan Sanstha (SS), 165–166, 171–172. *See also* Hindu right assassinations
Sangh Parivar, 21
Sastry, Subbaraya, 142–143
"Science of Aeronautics." *See Vymanika Shastra* (*VS*)
Sen, Shoma, 178, 187
Setalvad, Teesta, 26, 39, 126
Sevin, 49–51. *See also* Bhopal, 1984 industrial disaster; methyl isocyanate (MIC)
Shah, Amit, 36–37, 40, 90, 104–105, 167
Silent Spring (Carson), 49

Index

"Startup India." See Make in India
Swamy, Stan, 178, 186–187

Tagore, Rabindranath, 152
Talpade, Shivkar Bapuji, 150–152
Tanha, Asif Iqbal, 184–185
Teltumbde, Anand, 178–179, 181, 186
Trans-Asian Highway, 63, 73–74, 82

Union Carbide: establishment in India of, 48; Indian government's support of, 50–51; promotion of Sevin by, 49–51. See also Bhopal, 1984 industrial disaster; Dow Chemical Company
Union Carbide, Bhopal factory: lack of safety measures at, 51–53, 51n; local protests over, 51; present-day contamination of, 57; present-day description of, 53–54; production of methyl isocyanate (MIC) at, 50–51
Union Carbide Karamchari Sangh (Workers' Union), 51n
Unlawful Activities Prevention Act (UAPA): lack of false imprisonment compensation under, 189–190; as used to target activists, 175, 179; as used to target opposition to Narendra Modi, 189; as used to target protesters, 184

Vedic aircraft. See vimanas
Vibrant Gujarat. See Gujarat model
vimanas, 140, 150
Vishwa Hindu Parishad, 22, 112. See also Indian diaspora
Vivekananda, 18–19, 111
Vyapam scam, 167. See also Hindu right assassinations

Vymanika Shastra (*VS*): content of, 141, 145–146; creation of, 142–143; criticisms of, 145–146; current context of, 148–149; historical context of, 146–147; militarism in, 146; publication of, 143–144. See also Hindu nationalism, mythmaking

Wadud, Aman, 91–94
war on terror, 4, 27–28, 38, 177, 179. See also Unlawful Activities Prevention Act (UAPA)
West: exploitation of India by, 153; ignorance of, 2, 4; as Narendra Modi's accomplice, 5–6, 13–15, 29–30; view of India as ally by, 4, 32
Wilson, Rona: arrest of, 175; campaigning for political prisoners by, 176; manufactured evidence against, 178, 181
World Is Flat, The (Friedman), 32–33

Zona (Dyer), 45

About the Author

Born in Shillong, northeastern India, Siddhartha Deb lives in Harlem, New York. His fiction and nonfiction have been longlisted for the International Dublin Literary Award, shortlisted for the Orwell Prize, and been awarded the Pen Open prize. His journalism and essays have appeared in the *New York Times*, the *Guardian*, the *New Republic, Dissent, The Baffler, N+1*, and *Caravan*. His latest novel, *The Light at the End of the World*, was published in 2023 by Soho Press.

About Haymarket Books

Haymarket Books is a radical, independent, nonprofit book publisher based in Chicago. Our mission is to publish books that contribute to struggles for social and economic justice. We strive to make our books a vibrant and organic part of social movements and the education and development of a critical, engaged, and internationalist Left.

We take inspiration and courage from our namesakes, the Haymarket Martyrs, who gave their lives fighting for a better world. Their 1886 struggle for the eight-hour day—which gave us May Day, the international workers' holiday—reminds workers around the world that ordinary people can organize and struggle for their own liberation. These struggles—against oppression, exploitation, environmental devastation, and war—continue today across the globe.

Since our founding in 2001, Haymarket has published more than nine hundred titles. Radically independent, we seek to drive a wedge into the risk-averse world of corporate book publishing. Our authors include Angela Y. Davis, Arundhati Roy, Keeanga-Yamahtta Taylor, Eve Ewing, Aja Monet, Mariame Kaba, Naomi Klein, Rebecca Solnit, Olúfẹ́mi O. Táíwò, Mohammed El-Kurd, José Olivarez, Noam Chomsky, Winona LaDuke, Robyn Maynard, Leanne Betasamosake Simpson, Howard Zinn, Mike Davis, Marc Lamont Hill, Dave Zirin, Astra Taylor, and Amy Goodman, among many other leading writers of our time. We are also the trade publishers of the acclaimed Historical Materialism Book Series.

Haymarket also manages a vibrant community organizing and event space in Chicago, Haymarket House, the popular Haymarket Books Live event series and podcast, and the annual Socialism Conference.

www.ingramcontent.com/pod-product-compliance
Lightning Source LLC
Jackson TN
JSHW021904080625
85732JS00001B/2